How Disruption Brought Order

How Disruption Brought Order

The Story of a Winning Strategy in the
World of Advertising

Jean-Marie Dru

CEO, TBWA Worldwide

HOW DISRUPTION BROUGHT ORDER
Copyright © Jean-Marie Dru, 2007.

First published in 2007 by
PALGRAVE MACMILLAN™
175 Fifth Avenue, New York, N.Y. 10010 and
Houndmills, Basingstoke, Hampshire, England RG21 6XS
Companies and representatives throughout the world.

PALGRAVE MACMILLAN is the global academic imprint of the Palgrave Macmillan division of St. Martin's Press, LLC and of Palgrave Macmillan Ltd. Macmillan® is a registered trademark in the United States, United Kingdom and other countries. Palgrave is a registered trademark in the European Union and other countries.

ISBN-13: 978–0–230–60069–0
ISBN-10: 0–230–60069–7

Library of Congress Cataloging-in-Publication Data

Dru, Jean-Marie.
    How disruption brought order : the story of a winning strategy in the world of advertising / Jean-Marie Dru.
        p. cm.
    Includes bibliographical references and index.
    ISBN 0–230–60069–7
        1. Advertising agencies. 2. Advertising—Cross-cultural studies.
    3. TWBA (Firm). I. Title.

HG6178.D782 2007
659.1'11—dc22   2007016216

A catalogue record for this book is available from the British Library.

Design by Newgen Imaging Systems (P) Ltd., Chennai, India.

First edition: September 2007

10 9 8 7 6 5 4 3 2 1

Printed in the United States of America.

To René
To Marie-Virginie

Blessed.

I do not think that I could find a better word to describe how I have felt over the past seven years as a result of having the good fortune to know and work with Lee Clow. We share the same passions, the same respect for the business we are in, and the same desire to change things.

To near the end of my career in partnership with him, one of the most inspired advertising men in this industry, makes me truly grateful.

Lee adopted Disruption from the first day, and every day I am overwhelmed by his creative talent. His presence is felt every living second, in every corner of our company. He gives us all the energy to constantly aim for the high ground.

He is a legend.

Contents

How Disruption Brought Order

Introduction

It finds its way into our business meetings. It punctuates our speech, shapes our way of thinking, and guides our company's direction. It imbues our journey with a scent of adventure, leads us down unexpected paths, and spreads from city to city with a complete disregard for borders. At the same time, it troubles and comforts us. It makes our company a different kind of place, and we cannot do without it.

It is a word that sounds ungraceful but has burrowed itself into the heart of our agency. Of Latin origin, it is a word that the French introduced into the English language and that subsequently disappeared from French. It signifies "rupture," or rather the act of "creating a rupture." The word is *disruption*.

In our agency, we define Disruption as breaking with the status quo, refusing given wisdom, and finding unexpected solutions. We are not talking about gradual change or marginal evolution. We believe that the best way to help our clients grow their businesses is most often through strategies that involve a rupture.

And we have been fortunate enough to work with clients who share this belief, clients who are icons, who are transforming the businesses they are in—Apple, Absolut, Sony, Nissan, Mars and Nivea, among others.

As a methodology, Disruption is a three-step process: Convention, Disruption, and Vision. You start by identifying the Conventions that restrict the thought processes, and then you challenge them through a Disruption, a radically new approach. This is all done with a very definite sense of Vision—of where you are going, of the ground you want to cover from today to tomorrow.

This method did not come along by accident. It was, and remains, the result of an attitude, a mindset, an anti-establishment culture. We like to do things differently. We would even go so far as to say that it is the only path to survival. We like to use the words "question," "object," "contradict," "challenge," "contest," "disapprove," and the like.

This contradictory spirit, often considered a fault on an individual level, becomes a virtue when it is expressed collectively.

PART I

Thinking Differently

The Method

(Or Why Our Way of Working Makes Our Agency a Different Kind of Company)

If you look at the list of the top advertising networks worldwide, the only newcomer in the past ten years is TBWA. It was the fruit of several mergers. Among the most memorable of these were the absorptions of Chiat/Day and, later, BDDP. Born in Paris, BDDP is an agency I co-founded in 1984. There we invented the Disruption methodology. Parallelly, Chiat/Day, born in Los Angeles, is probably the agency with the most disruptive spirit in America, perhaps the world. This is the agency that became famous around the globe that same year in 1984, with the campaign for the launch of the Macintosh computer.

These agencies were made for each other. Following their merger, resources were pooled, cultures were blended, ways of doing things were mixed; this gave a new energy to the company that is now known as TBWA.

All the agencies TBWA now encompasses were founded by real entrepreneurs, and a large number of them are still with us. This has resulted in an impressive group of talented people, a group that our competitors admired, a group of creative people whose reputation has gone well beyond their original frontiers: first and foremost Lee Clow from Los Angeles, John Hunt from Johannesburg, and Trevor Beattie from London.

But we soon realized that talented individuals alone were not enough to build a successful network and to create something truly different in our industry. We needed a catalyst, something for these talents to rally around and to bring us inexorably together.

I offered Disruption.

At first, the concept was rejected. The method and its underlying culture were too closely linked to one of the agencies that had been absorbed. The buyer rarely embraces the culture of the acquired. Because I did not want to force Disruption on people, I thought it was going to disappear.

Months passed. Then John Hunt of South Africa invented a brilliant new way of conducting Disruption Days, and he started to share his new expertise with people from other countries. Sometime later, one of our board members finally stated the obvious: "We are really stupid not to realize that Disruption is the idea."

From that moment on, Disruption became the mantra of our company. It was consistent with Lee Clow's swashbuckling pirate flag, with the irreverence of Trevor Beattie, and with the unorthodox approach of John Hunt.

Once we had a unifying philosophy, a rallying cry, once everybody started to buy into it, I knew we could create something special. In this book, I would like to tell the story of Disruption and all it has done, in the hope that it might inspire others who are seeking to create change in their own companies.

UNFAIR COMPETITIVE ADVANTAGE

Disruption is fed by the idea of change. In theory, we are all in favor of change. But the truth is that each of us is most at ease in the comfort of the status quo.

Yet the only thing that you can be sure of is that if you stay still, you will fail. I often use this quote by Paul Valéry: "We need to wake up from a thought that lasts too long." Companies and brands that do not try to see and do things in a new way find their personalities gradually diminishing. Our job is to help them to constantly renew themselves.

Hunt/Lascaris is the agency in our group that knows better than any other how to borrow from others. Whatever the project, idea, or suggestion, John Hunt captures it, takes it on board, revises it, and comes up with a new and completely transformed initiative. In *Disruption*, the book I published in the mid-1990s, I briefly described our intention to organize brainstorming sessions around Disruption, a topic I termed *Disruption Days*. From this embryo of an idea, John Hunt and Marie Jamieson, the agency's planning director, created a complete process for Disruption Days, a brainstorming program between clients and the agency that has proved incredibly rewarding. Three chapters of a compilation book entitled *Beyond Disruption*, published in 2002, show how Disruption Days are put into practice.

For a long time, these Disruption Days followed the usual Disruption sequence: Convention, Disruption, Vision. The method then evolved over the course of the hundreds of Disruption

Days we have organized for our clients. We always begin with a detailed analysis of Conventions—in other words, the assumptions and given wisdom that apply to a market or a brand—but we then go straight toward defining the Vision, a new way for the brand or a company to imagine its future. Work on Disruption becomes the third phase, with Disruption being defined as "the idea that will accelerate our journey from the challenged convention to the renewed vision."

Though we may not define a ten-year plan each and every time, we always come up with something: a new product idea, an innovative way of seeing the brand portfolio, an original approach to retail, and so on. This allows the agency to begin a dialogue on another level from that of a typical creative presentation. On occasion, young executives from our clients have come down to my office in New York to tell me that, thanks to Disruption, they could finally express their opinions and have their voices heard.

For TBWA, Disruption has become a decisive advantage. Our method allows us to be creative not only at the final creative stage, but also in the initial strategic stages. We believe in being creative before the creative process starts. As for Disruption Days, they create levels of proximity and communication with our clients that some thought was impossible today.

I recently came across what I had written about this method in 1996: "Disruption is a catalyst for the imagination, a guide that opens up many paths, a method that allows us to turn perspectives inside out, a process that breathes new life into brands, an alternative to standard ways of thinking. In a word, Disruption is an agent of change."

And this is what Carisa Bianchi, president of our Los Angeles office, our largest agency, had to say on the subject: "Make no mistake, Disruption won all our recent pitches. We made an active choice to unleash the power of Disruption early and often. Disruption is a tangible asset that makes a tangible difference. It puts us on a different level. It inspires us to excel and gives us an unfair competitive advantage."

A WORLDWIDE TOUR OF DISRUPTION

Our first Disruption dates back to the 1980s. It concerned a little-known sports watch brand that has gone on to become a famous luxury brand. In the space of three years, the average price of a Tag Heuer watch went from $600 to $1,500. To raise the brand's status, the campaign had to raise the status of sport and the athlete. Tag Heuer highlighted the fact that in sport, as in all competitive activities, mental strength is what makes the difference.

In the campaign, an athlete conjured up imaginary obstacles in his mind in order to push himself farther; we used a stick of dynamite for a relay runner or a razor blade in place of a hurdle. Imagination became a source of motivation. The concept, elaborated on in the slogan *Don't Crack under Pressure,* bridged the gap between sport and prestige, between sweat and luxury, making it a true Disruption.

When I am asked to give a recent example, I often cite what we have done for Nextel. The case is very demonstrative in its sheer simplicity. Nextel's Disruption can be summed up in a few words: *Others talk, we do*.

We described Nextel as the company of *doers*. The majority of its customers were initially blue-collar workers, for instance in the construction business. People with heavy workloads, people who have little time to waste. Our objective was to broaden Nextel's user base and to make its clients feel that they belonged to an exclusive club of *doers*. In reality, the message was targeted at anyone considering him or herself an entrepreneur, whatever the domain.

Defying all logic, a telecommunications company insinuated that things would be better if we spent less time talking and more time doing, even though the company's financial results depended on the amount of time its clients spent communicating. The strength of the campaign lies within this paradox. Overnight, Nextel was seen in a different light. Advertising defined the space it could occupy . . . The following year's annual report was entitled *"Ready. Set. Done."* Each section incorporated the word *do* or *done* in one form or another. The section dedicated to its mission was defined as follows: "We may be in the wireless communications market, but our mission is to help people talk less and do more."

We have identified four types of Disruptions in general and regrouped them into four concentric circles. Business is found at the center, with Advertising at the outermost circle. More precisely, the center is assigned to the business model, or how the company makes money. The second circle is devoted to the products and services it offers. The third is for marketing, that is to say, how these products or services are proposed to consumers. The last circle is that of Advertising. Disruption can intervene at any of these levels. The closer the Disruption is to the center, the more solid and durable it is, by definition.

In the first circle, Ikea and Amazon best illustrate companies that have invented different business models. As for the second circle, what company better than Apple represents companies consistently proposing revolutionary products? The Body Shop and Absolut are exemplary illustrations of marketing approaches that create a rupture in the third circle. Last but not least, Tag Heuer and Nextel show us how a Disruption at the communication level, supposedly the least enduring circle, can also create a powerful force.

In recent years, Disruption has spread across our network, to the four corners of the earth. I will describe in detail later in this book what we have created in the United States for Apple, Nissan, and Adidas. Their communication programs have been encapsulated in one word or sentence: *Think Different* for Apple, *Shift* for Nissan, and *Impossible Is Nothing* for Adidas. Each of these corporate taglines has inspired a series of disruptive initiatives. I will also show that in France, our actions have a profound effect on two institutions that you could not imagine more different: McDonald's, and the French Railways.

But first, let us look beyond the United States and France, at a number of unconventional strategies that have blossomed around the world. We will briefly examine a number of them, coming from ten different countries, starting with South Africa.

Our agency in Johannesburg lashed out at those who were banishing HIV-positive victims from their own villages in the bush, calling this behavior *the new Apartheid*. By retouching old black-and-white photos of "whites only" signs into signs saying "non-AIDS only," the agency took a stand against this new form of segregation. We exploited the most painful images from South Africa's collective consciousness to serve a noble cause. Quite disruptive.

The same agency recommended that Nando's, the fast food brand, raise its game with a delicious manipulation of the political agenda, registering itself as N.A.N.D.O.S, the New African National Democratic Organization for Solidarity, a new independent political party for the 2004 elections. One of the advantages of this new political party status was to obtain free advertising space in the mainstream press for campaigning: unbelievable but true.

Until recently, pharmacies in Sweden did not give advice to customers, but rather merely filled doctors' prescriptions. The goal of a recent advertising campaign was to train pharmacists on how to give advice on illness prevention, and in the process save millions of dollars worth of unnecessary time wasted in visits to doctors and sick leave. The seriousness of the subject did not inhibit the agency's creativity. Far from it. To promote oral hygiene, pharmacists were persuaded to organize a nationwide competition for the world's longest kiss, a category that is now recorded in the Guinness Book of World Records.

In Guatemala, an inexpensive motorcycle brand coming from India has trumped the big Japanese companies by making a virtue out of buying and using a motorbike not for fun or sport, but for work. As the advertisement says: *The motorbike helps you to do your job better*. As a result, the banks give preferential loans for the brand, which now enjoys more than 60 percent of the market. What was once cool—to own a Japanese brand—is now seen as a foolish waste of money.

We recommended that the United Kingdom's No. 1 garden retailer adopt a new vision, *to transform the* health *of every garden in Britain*. The competition's approach has always been merely cosmetic, horticultural "plastic surgery." These competitors were dealing only with the outer appearance, which indeed is the usual convention of the market. In making health the focus for all of its client's new garden products and services, the company saw itself in a different way. And its market share more than doubled in just two years.

The strategy we proposed to one of the largest insurance companies in Belgium consisted not just in selling insurance, but also in working with clients to reduce the very need for it. One of the company's recent new products is automobile insurance with lower premiums for those who go to work by train rather than driving their car. At the end of the day, if we launch more products like this, we can gradually participate in reconfiguring this client's business model from top to bottom.

Many people believe—incorrectly—that giving up smoking diminishes their ability to concentrate. In a Japanese chewing gum campaign, the concept of mind sharpening was expressed as a behavioral insight, *Chewing is thinking*. These three words are now the signature of our campaign, which fights a cultural taboo against chewing gum in the workplace.

One of our agencies in Spain discovered how to convince more companies to outsource work to prison workshops. They decided to make the label *Made in Prison* fashionable. To do this, they focused the spotlight on what had previously been hidden. It is now trendy to show that you are supporting Reinsertion Initiatives. "Made in Prison" has become the stamp of a cool fashion brand.

In Finland, the increase in domestic abuse had become a major national issue. Victims' shame drove them to invent stories of mishaps and clumsiness to explain their injuries. By wrapping warning tape on walls, steps, doors, table corners, and other areas of the home, we drew attention to the obvious dangers these everyday so-called hazards represented to women as a source of potential injury. This was a surprising way of executing an insightful strategy: When you choose to accept the lie from a victim of domestic abuse, you become a partner in the crime itself.

South Korea is one of the most sophisticated wireless telecommunications environments in the world. Despite this, our client, SK

Telecom, refused to participate in the prevalent hype around convergence. Instead of advertising the supposed joys of watching live sporting events on your phone, we did just the opposite. We invited customers to share all the reasons why SK Telecom is important to them in their lives, celebrating unexpected or very basic uses such as being able to check your lipstick, or setting your morning alarm call. Thousands of customers contributed their stories, which were featured on the web and also published in the most traditional of "analog" formats, a hardcover, modern handbook on daily life. The book was called "365 days."

When is a soup not a soup? When it is a snack alternative to coffee or tea in the office. Our disruptive marketing strategy chose to take a soup brand out of the cupboard at home and to place it in dispensers and vending machines in offices throughout the Netherlands. We took the brand to work, literally. Inspired by research that showed that the average worker's energy drops significantly in the afternoon, we created a new institution: 4:00 p.m. was a good time for a break—and a cup of soup. By positioning the product as the answer to a loss in business productivity, we recast the brand's role.

All these examples serve to show how Disruption has spread around our company. Each of our offices practices it daily. Above all, they all illustrate what is at the very heart of Disruption, which is to generate ideas at the strategic level. We want there to be an idea in the Disruption strategy itself. When this happens, the force of the creative product, the power of the words and images that translate the strategy, are greatly multiplied.

Disruption, the book, was published in 1996. In an advertisement published in the *Wall Street Journal*, I explained some ideas that are still at the heart of Disruption in action today: "From now on there can be no change without rupture; change is discontinuity. Consequently, gradual evolutions and series of adjustments are not enough. . . . What has changed, and is decisive in our eyes, is our conviction that what in the past was the fruit of intuition and chance must now be the basis of a systematic approach."

A quote that I often use in my speeches is from the well-known words of Benjamin Franklin: "Insanity is doing the same thing over and over again, expecting something different to happen." Most of the people I speak to start to smile when I say this, forgetting that, more often than not, it is aimed directly at them.

"DISRUPTION DAYS"

Peter Drucker wrote thirty-five books on management during his long career, including numerous best-sellers. Over twenty years ago now, he wrote: "Creative destruction needs to be an ongoing process, and it has to be organized." This is exactly what Disruption is aiming for, remaining an open system that is constantly enriched by each person's experience. It is about a process that can be entered at the beginning or at the end, that can even be ignored in the initial stages, but subsequently serves as a benchmark to measure progress. It is a system for those who do not like systems. And this is what we wanted it to be. It is even adopted by our creative people who are normally bored to death by any sort of strategic format.

As for Disruption Days, they offer our clients a step-by-step approach of precise and innovative exercises. Just one example is when participants are invited to imagine the future of their company while wearing the hat of an innovative business leader, such as Steve Jobs or Richard Branson.

After being introduced in South Africa, our main offices gradually adopted these Disruption Days, starting with Los Angeles, our largest and most influential office. The L.A. adoption marked the turning point of Disruption, not least because one of this office's principal clients adopted the method right away. Today Disruption Days are organized every year in several cities across the world for the major brands we handle for the Mars company.

We have already organized no fewer than seven hundred Disruption Days across our network. By the time this book is published, the number will be close to a thousand. With fifteen to twenty clients attending each session, nearly fifteen thousand client individuals have now taken part. Almost each one has asked to continue the experience.

A typical Disruption Day goes as follows: morning welcome, introduction to Disruption and timetable, warm-up exercises, identifying Conventions, exploring Visions. Then comes lunch, followed by question-and-answer games, role-play, "what-if" exercises, voting and evaluating Disruptions, recap of the day, and conclusion.

Identifying Conventions allows us to answer the question "How did we get here?" Of course, the objective of Disruption Days is to come up with Disruptions, but often the longest part of the exercise consists in bringing Conventions out into the open, helping our clients to recognize them and stimulating their desire to challenge them.

The approach begins with the systematic analysis of everything that appears to be conventional in a given market. Instead of looking for differences, we concentrate on looking for commonalities. And when commonalities have been discovered, there may be conventions to be broken.

Work on Conventions is always productive. We all tend to pay attention to the same things, but also to disregard the same things. We are collectively blind in the same way.

The second part of the morning, exploring Visions, is dedicated to answering the question: "Where do we want to go? What do we want to be five years from now?" We go forward in time and try to imagine which of the possible futures might materialize for the brand or the company. Examining this array of possibilities allows us to break away from a linear way of thinking and helps us avoid simply contradicting Conventions when creating a Vision for the brand or the company.

In the afternoon we conduct various exercises, including a round of "what-if" sessions. This identity-switching exercise is aimed at breaking down the inhibitions linked to our clients' corporate culture. We engage participants in role-playing. For an hour or two, as mentioned, they become Richard Branson or Steve Jobs. They have to think like that person. This encourages them to think up radical strategies, notions that could not even have been mentioned up until that point. We revisit each convention, wearing the "hat" of another company: How would Virgin attack my market? Changing identities in this manner always generates unusual ideas.

We have a break after these exercises in order to go back to the Vision. We begin to refine what was written during the morning session in light of the disruptive ideas generated at the beginning of the afternoon. The after influences the before, the execution influences the idea. This inversion of the normal sequence is one of the foundations of Disruption as a method.

We call the final exercise "headline." It involves imagining the perfect title for an article appearing one year later in *The Wall Street*

Journal or *The Financial Times*, describing the new successful initiatives taken by the company. These articles are laudatory. Group members have to determine what they will have accomplished to merit such an honor. This exercise is our imaginary way of summing up the progress made over the course of the day.

Each sequence in the day is accompanied by a vote. The moderator pins up several points to summarize what has been accomplished so far, and orient the way the exercises are organized. A few days later, our agency writes a document reporting on the entire day and giving recommendations on the routes that the client should follow.

In most companies, those responsible for strategy are found at the top of the management structure. They are rarely young, which is a pity, as it is precisely the young who have the most to win or lose in the future. In response to the criticism that they lack experience, we say: Naturally, but isn't the lack of maturity of the vast majority preferable to the lack of imagination of a select few? Thanks to Disruption and the votes that punctuate it, a process is started that gives rise to new strategies that bypass hierarchy. We are starting to experience what Gary Hamel, author of the book *Competing for the Future*, referred to as "democratization of the strategy." Tomorrow it will be the key to success for the most creative companies.

I read a paper on Silicon Valley the other day that described it as a place devoid of nostalgia. "It is no longer a place," wrote the journalist, "but rather a metaphor for unrestrained imagination, constant experimentation and total lack of nostalgia." In the space of only a few hours, a Disruption Day sweeps away the debris of the past for participants. During this short amount of time, they take leave of what they know, and use the past to guide the future instead of remaining frozen within it.

The exercises we conceive encourage *re-creation*, which is a word linked in its origins to *creation*. As the day advances, people become more and more enthusiastic in sensing the progress that is being made. To achieve this progress, everything is important, from the way the questions are asked, to how people are divided into groups, to the amount of time dedicated to each workshop, even to where the day takes place. We recently organized a Disruption Day in an old Russian church converted into an Italian restaurant by an Irishman in Shanghai.

A SHARE OF THE FUTURE

Disruption is in tune with our times, this world of fierce global competition, of shortening cycles, and of constant turbulence. In such an unstable context, brands must evolve permanently to stay relevant. We try to give clear directions, to give our clients a sense of increased control, despite ever stronger pressures. We talk about "share of future," not "share of market." Brands change. We deal with change.

A few years ago, I summed up this issue in this way:

If you change nothing within a company you are sure to fail. As you also will if you try to change everything. The key to success lies within your ability to determine the fine line between what must change and what must not. The same applies to the brand. All brands are in a constant state of transition. It is impossible to build brands by thinking in mere linear terms. You must imagine greater futures for them. You need to call upon your imagination in order to achieve this. Which is where Disruption comes into play, and its role in the discovery of new futures.

As Bob Dylan said: "We are constantly in a state of becoming."

Disruption has given us tools, a vocabulary, a point of view. It stimulates ideas that are bigger than those that could only apply to advertising. It crosses boundaries. It stimulates and federates all communications disciplines, without exception. It has affirmed itself through the books dedicated to it that have been sold all over the world. It is also the philosophy that guides the way we manage our company. This led *Campaign*, the leading British trade press magazine, to choose a paradoxical title to describe the ground covered by our company over the last five years: "How Disruption Brought Order."

In fact, we behave more as catalysts than solution providers. We do not seek out solutions ourselves; we help our clients to find them, because a company that has defined its own problem and imagined the solution to it has a far better chance of success.

Whether it is an idea that aims to change the world, or a more modest idea intended to change how we think of a brand, whatever the subject, noble or trivial, important or less so, Disruption has its part to play. It helps transform the brands we handle by making their clients, the consumers, see them in a different light, giving them more meaning.

I have chosen three examples to develop. One explains the change in Pedigree's advertising, the other shows us how McDonald's now manages its brand in France, the third describes how the SNCF, the French Railways, has "put the client back at the center," as we say today.

Advertising, brand, client. These cases cover the three main concerns of the advertising professional.

FROM RATIONAL TO EMOTIONAL

When we first met in 2002, the chief executive officer of the Mars Company, Paul Michaels, told us: "We want to be the most disruptive consumer goods company in the world." We were amazed to hear the word "disruptive" come from his mouth before we had even mentioned it.

We started working with his company just after the meeting. And since then, we have been more and more involved, working on a growing number of brands. Later, Paul Michaels awarded us the Pedigree account, Mars's biggest brand.

We like to believe that we helped influence the way Pedigree's employees felt about their company. We organized a series of Disruption Days during the summer of 2004, lasting for a period of two months. The agency had already managed these sorts of workshop with other clients, but never on an international scale such as this. Intensive seminars took place all over the world, in London, Warsaw, Bangkok, Tokyo, São Paolo, Shanghai, and Los Angeles.

Our Mars client invited over two hundred managers to participate in the process, coming from all corners of the globe. Each day we immersed ourselves in the images, language, packaging, odors, tastes, and anything else associated with dogs and their nutrition.

What surfaced was an acute realization of a terrible sameness. Each campaign showed us dogs wagging their tails at the sight of their next meal, with the product falling into their bowl in slow motion.

And yet these conventional images hide a much deeper truth. People have real feelings for their dogs. One survey shows that half of all American dog owners include their pet in their family portraits.

We can observe similar types of behavior in other countries, even in developing markets where dog food is not yet widespread. How ever people may feed their dogs, their attachment knows no limits. Dog lovers love and respect their dogs in all their "dogginess."

The agency conceived a phrase that, in time, revealed itself much richer than at first glance: *For the love of dogs* would become the manifesto of the company and the thought behind the future campaign. No other producer had yet adopted the stance of defender of dogs. Given its history as a pioneer, Pedigree was in a perfect position to take this direction. In fact, it was almost an obligation.

The agency recommended that the company produce a document available to all employees that would make them aware of the extent of the change taking place and to invite their participation. The document imagined was in the form of a book, a manifesto called *Dogma*. It went on to become the company bible in the transitional period that was to come.

Dogma set down in black and white the faith that Pedigree would inspire from that point onward:

> We're for dogs.
> Some people are for the whales,
> Some are for the trees . . .
> The big ones and the little ones,
> The guardians and the comedians,
> The pure breeds and the mutts.
> We're for walks, runs, and romps,
> Digging, scratching, sniffing and fetching,
> We're for dog parks, dog doors and dog days,
> If there were an international holiday for dogs

on which all dogs were universally recognized
for the quality of their contribution to our lives,
we'd be for that too.
Because we're for dogs.

This manifesto was then revealed to the general public as part of an advertising campaign. Presenting it to its employees first was a way for Pedigree to prepare the groundwork.

In the foreword, Paul Michaels suggested that *Dogma* be used "like a compass to find one's way and take daily decisions, like a breath of fresh air for difficult days and as an easy way of showing friends and family what it is like to work for Pedigree." He summed everything up in this simple phrase: "Everything that we do, we do for the love of dogs."

Pedigree went on to initiate a series of changes. Life at the company changed overnight. Every office was redesigned to welcome employees' dogs, whether in flesh and blood or in photos on the walls and on business cards. In several countries, managers even asked sales representatives to take their dogs with them when they toured supermarkets. All of this was not as simple as it might seem. In Japan, the company was housed in a building where dogs were forbidden.

Another idea came out of one of these Disruption Days: Pedigree's launch of a health insurance program for its employees' dogs. This made the company a model to follow, and key players in the market were quick to follow suit.

It was at this moment that the new campaign slogan appeared, encapsulating how true dog lovers feel in just two words: *Dogs Rule.* The profession of faith laid down in the book was repeated in the voice-over of a spot showing ordinary dogs living their daily lives: digging holes, sniffing around, doing what all dogs do. And because dogs love to go out for walks above all else, the campaign went out with them, carrying their photos on strategically placed giant posters.

From that point onward, everything that Pedigree did would be done "for the love of dogs." This expression acted as a template, to inform all decisions concerning the brand. The change was remarkable, the difference loud and clear. The Tokyo branch finally moved its entire staff to new offices, the ultimate proof of the company's commitment.

Mars eventually adopted Disruption to the point of making it one of its internal methodologies. Disruption Days are now part of the company. We have organized them in over fifteen cities for brands as diverse as Pedigree, Whiskas, Skittles, Sheba, Snickers, Uncle Ben's, and Seeds of Change. In the words of John Hunt, Mars was the first in a number of our clients to become a *serial disruptor*.

These clients carry out Disruption Days on a regular basis. They shift the parameters each time, resolve a problem, explore an opportunity, rapidly moving on to implementation stage, before organizing a new Disruption Day to stretch their thinking yet further. Little by little, this has all led to Disruption becoming part of the way these companies think about their business.

FROM BRAND TO COMPANY

I do not think that Denis Hennequin and Jean-Pierre Petit would object to me also describing them as serial disruptors. They were so before the word "Disruption" even came on to the scene. Hennequin is president of McDonald's Europe, Petit, of McDonald's Southern Europe. Their successful careers have without a doubt been helped by the performance of the French McDonald's operation, the only one within the major markets to have witnessed uninterrupted growth over the last ten years. It is also the operation that has proposed and implemented unconventional solutions, even disruptive strategies, the most systematically. Hennequin and Petit have achieved the rarest thing, turning the French "exception" into an example that others would eventually follow.

It all started in 1997, when McDonald's found itself in the midst of a trade war between the United States and Europe, with the American government attempting to protect the interests of its farmers. A short while later, José Bové, a French farmer turned politician and antiglobalization leader, organized a raid on a McDonald's restaurant under construction in the small town of Millau, not far from his home. In France, McDonald's had become the scapegoat for all the ills of the modern-day world, of globalization and the supposed unlimited economic power of multinationals. The irony in McDonald's case was that the company sourced 78 percent of its food products from French farmers and over 99 percent from Europe.

The point of no return came in April 2000, when a small group of extremists set off a homemade bomb in a restaurant in Brittany, killing an employee. The morning papers published a statement saying "Enough is enough." It was the first time that McDonald's had communicated at a corporate level. Up until that point, the company had tended to hide behind the brand. The French loved the brand and what went with it—Happy Meals, Ronald, the "Best of" menus, and so on—but were wary of the company itself. This tragic event in Brittany acted as a catalyst for change. From then onwards, McDonald's was going to make sure that the public had a very clear idea of what was going on behind its doors. The company felt it was time to come out into the open.

In 2000 McDonald's opened the debate on the BSE crisis, otherwise known as mad cow disease, before it had even hit the headlines. It took courage to be the first to broach the subject. Most executives in other companies, concerned by the same issues, were tempted to hope that the crisis would go away, rather than having what it took to tackle it head on. McDonald's went public with a very simple message: "You are right to be concerned about BSE; here are the facts . . ." The public reacted very positively. McDonald's low public profile was gone forever.

In the same vein, the company organized a series of open days in 2001, allowing both the public and the media to visit the kitchens of its restaurants, company headquarters, suppliers' offices, even the advertising agency.

The year 2002 saw the company partnering with the agricultural industry. In May a charter was launched detailing the mutual commitments of farmers and McDonald's in terms of traceability, sanitary controls, respect for the environment, and the respectful treatment of animals. That year McDonald's reserved a stand at the agriculture trade fair. The initiative could have been taken as a provocation, coming not so long after Millau, but it was actually very well received.

A spot about the four seasons accompanied the various programs. Successive frames showed a wheat field, tomatoes being cultivated, a bull grazing in a meadow, lettuce growing. Each scene was subtitled: "nine months," "one hundred and twenty days," "five years," "eighty-five days". . . . The voice-over began the moment we saw these products being transformed or cooked: "Nature has its own rhythm, and so do we. To reconcile each of them, we have developed a program of best practice with our partners in the agricultural world. Because every day, we strive to satisfy your desires. At your rhythm."

This willingness to open up has undeniably changed the way the public sees the McDonald's company, including its role as an employer. Numerous initiatives have been undertaken for the young. These include the implementation of new, thoughtfully designed employment contracts that have transformed the image of the "McJob," which for a long time had been synonymous with instability, low wages, low skills, and a lack of career prospects. Working at "McDo," as teenagers call it in France, has gradually evolved into a respectable first job, opening the door to the employment market.

A corporate advertising campaign also put these initiatives into perspective. The first film was set in a university library. Two students were at a computer consulting a job website. They lamented that the market had only temporary jobs to offer. One was complaining, while the other reassured him that we all have to start somewhere. The voice-over commented: "At McDonald's, 80 percent of our staff are given full-time contracts the moment they are hired."

The second film showed a student hugging his girlfriend, explaining how difficult it was to fit his study hours around working to support himself. He even considered giving up his studies. His girlfriend tried to talk him out of it, especially given the fact that he was a good student. The voice-over concluded: "At McDonald's, almost 50 percent of our team members are students who can adjust their work hours in order to continue their studies."

In the third film, two young employees were chatting in an office. The first wanted to know if his friend had finally managed to get his promotion. The second replied that he would have to wait a bit longer because he was still "a little young." His friend said that he had been waiting long enough and that it was time to be more insistent. The voice-off answered: "At McDonald's, the average promotion age to manager is twenty-seven. A manager oversees ten to fifteen people."

In 2005, when suburban rioting echoed the frustrations of today's youth, the company reacted immediately by going public with its commitments and employment policy. McDonald's recruits a lot of young people, many coming from the areas where the riots had sparked.

The company's subsequent online recruitment program had an immediate boost, recording almost seventeen thousand résumé postings per week. The press covered each and every one of these initiatives. In March 2006 *Management* magazine ran with the headline: "McDo the pioneer of 'Black, blanc, beur' recruitment." In France, home of the "Bleu, blanc, rouge," this alliteration describes the cultural diversity made up of people of black, white, and Arab origin. The following month, the same publication ranked McDonald's the eighth best company to work for and number one in terms of opportunities for promotion and job security. The public began to realize that McDonald's created real openings for young people, not just last-resort jobs.

To achieve such results, McDonald's France had to create a number of ruptures within the McDonald's system. These Disruptions subsequently became benchmarks for other markets, starting with China.

For the last three years, the Chinese population has been faced with a number of food crises that have sown seeds of doubt regarding the quality of meat products: SARS, foot-and-mouth disease, bird flu. So many worrying issues coupled with a lack of governmental information has allowed people's imaginations to run riot. The McDonald's business in China was hard hit by this anxiety-producing context. Chinese mothers, who most often have only one child, their "little emperor," tended to distrust Western foods and turn toward more traditional recipes instead.

A Disruption Day was organized in Beijing, bringing together the key stakeholders from the Chinese company as well as two representatives from our Paris agency. The objective was to draw up a plan capable of proving the quality of the foods McDonald's offers. It should be said that McDonald's showed an unrivaled attention to quality in China. For example, no less that five years were spent on the acclimation of a potato variety selected by McDonald's before the first fries went on sale in its restaurants.

Following this Disruption Day, a decision was made to launch a program inviting opinion leaders to come and see for themselves the extent to which McDonald's stood firm on quality issues: Factory visits, open days, partnerships with veterinary schools, and more were organized in close collaboration with regional governments. The aim was both to help government leaders to better understand each quality process, but also to convince them to integrate some of these programs into their own local public health activities. And they did. Later the health ministers of several provinces decided to visit the McDonald's headquarters in Chicago.

Let us now return to Europe, where problems of a similar nature had also manifested themselves. In the United Kingdom, for example, McDonald's had failed to fully anticipate the escalation of what we might refer to as food scares.

It all started in the mid-1980s with the battle between McDonald's and Greenpeace. McDonald's won its case in 1996, after a legal battle that had lasted several years, but it had lost the battle for public opinion. A traumatized McDonald's UK would hide away in a state of regrettable silence for several years, amid a crescendo of criticism. New accusations were added with every weekend that went by. The brand was even accused of being responsible for the deforestation of the Amazonian rain forests. Nutrition, food quality, child exploitation, "McJobs": Anything was fodder for the raging machine.

Given the context, McDonald's UK's responses were both too limited and defensive. At the same time that the Eric Schlosser book *Chew on This* was being distributed in schools, the *Guardian* decided to publish key extracts and gave away 600,000 copies of the *Supersize Me* DVD. The time had come to speak out.

The day the DVD was distributed, McDonald's bought a full-page ad in the *Guardian*, titled "Everything McDonald's does is questionable," playing on the double meaning of "questionable." Very few companies would have the courage to make such a statement, even admitting that they did not have all the answers. It was an open invitation for starting a dialogue. The advertisement carried both a telephone number and an e-mail address.

The following Monday, Steve Easterbrook, McDonald's UK president, made a new statement in the *Guardian*: "We are not saying we are perfect, and we are committed to constantly improving ourselves while continuing to listen to what our clients and other parties have to say, but we will not accept being made scapegoats, blamed for all the ills of today's society. It is time to take a look at who we really are and what we do to be a good burger company. All we ask is to be judged on the facts."

The political battle—that is the only way to describe it—had now begun in the United Kingdom. Public opinion had registered and appreciated this new transparency. As for company employees, it goes without saying that they felt vindicated by these stances.

Some people like McDonald's, others less so, but today, in the United Kingdom and everywhere else, people are grateful for this newfound openness, what I might call "corporate transparency." In each of the countries where McDonald's operates, the company has done more than just reply. It has anticipated, it has invented new ways of running the business, echoing Peter Drucker's famous aphorism: "The things we hear about adapting to change are not only stupid, they are dangerous. The only way of managing change is to create it."

FROM USER TO CLIENT

Another of our clients SNCF, the acronym for the French Railways, has brilliantly shown its way of managing change. Not so long ago it was not customary to use the word "clients" in our meetings with the SNCF. This is a state-owned company, which was not supposed to have clients, only users.

Considerable progress has been made since. The SNCF has gone beyond its status as a transport company to become a *service* company, serving its clients. It has managed to completely transform itself from the inward-facing company it once was, more preoccupied with its internal conflicts than its customers. It has changed to such an extent that it was even recently congratulated by a panel of journalists for the quality and regularity of the information it provided to its diverse public.

This evolution, which comes above all from the inside, can nevertheless be illustrated through the corporate slogans that have punctuated its communication over the last fifteen years, starting with *Le progrès ne vaut que s'il est partagé par tous* (Progress is worthless unless everybody has a share in it). This slogan, with nineteenth-century socialistic overtones, was launched at the same time as the high-speed train serving the west of France, the TGV Atlantic. The SNCF simply wanted to point out that thanks to the democratization of high-speed travel, the train had surpassed the plane in making breakthrough technology available to the masses.

A few years later the SNCF became definitively client-centric with the proclamation: *A nous de vous faire préférer le train* (It is up to us to make you prefer the train). With this "up to us" proclamation, it set itself a challenge that went far beyond a simple advertising formula.

At this point, the company launched a wide-reaching campaign called *commitments* to reinforce the slogan. It was a campaign that was simultaneously outward facing, to show the public that the SNCF wanted to and would change, and inward facing, to signal the change to SNCF personnel and lay out their responsibilities. The response from the unions, led by the CGT, the most left-wing of them all, was favorable, and they became actively involved in the initiative. Tens of thousands of questionnaires were filled out in stations by clients; thousands of rail workers participated in the operation by managing the process. The SNCF responded accordingly with a series of acts, these famous "commitments": train punctuality, information transparency, standards of cleanliness in stations and carriages, and the like.

The climax of the period was the launch of the Paris-to-London route. The fact that the English capital was a mere two and a half hours away from Paris had a profound effect on people's minds. Traveling abroad became accessible. Making Avignon two hours and forty minutes away from Paris was just as convenient. With Paris to London in two and a half hours, the SNCF had opened up a new world to us.

Increasing the frequency of trains and revising the tariff system were other ways to make people prefer rail travel. Over time, the SNCF made the train appealing to a broader public. It has become the uncontested rail leader in Europe and an outstanding example of a modern state-owned company.

Things had moved on. The mere idea of serving the client was no longer enough. What had not been understood ten years earlier was now a given. It was time to go one step further. The SNCF decided to develop a whole new panoply of ideas giving rise to the new slogan: *Donner au train des idées d'avance* (Giving the train ideas in advance). And so a number of services began to emerge, including Tikefone, allowing users to buy and store their ticket on their mobile telephone, DVD rentals in train stations, and the ability to download books from the SNCF website. The SNCF employees received information regarding incidents in real time on their mobile phones, with this same information being made available on the voyage-sncf.com website, a site not only offering train tickets, but also plane tickets, holidays, and short-break ideas. Today it has become the leading commercial site in France, all sectors considered, with a turnover of over 1 billion dollars.

We have now become accustomed to traveling from Paris to Lyon in two hours, to magazines being available on board the TGV, to "quiet areas," to improved facilities for people with impaired mobility, to train carriages decorated by Philippe Starck, to the students helping on rush-period days, to luggage delivery to the homes of the elderly, and much more besides. With its new slogan *ideas in advance*, the SNCF made a commitment to constantly innovate in order to improve the quality of its client service.

The Société Nationale des Chemins de Fer Français (SNCF) that was created in 1945, just after the war, had always been a part of French people's lives. It had accompanied them in so many moments and had grown up with them, subtly transforming itself into a modern-day company. It now represents a company at ease with its modernity, devoid of complexes, confident about a future that, with the help of Europe, is reaching out to it. What tracks have been covered!

Pedigree, McDonald's, the SNCF: Each is a prime example of a company that has managed to open itself up to new horizons by adopting groundbreaking strategies, taking unexpected initiatives, and coming up with original kinds of solutions. The aim of Disruption is to help our clients to give birth to some of these new ideas—not from time to time, but as part of a permanent process.

FOCAL POINT

Fiona Clancy is our worldwide strategic director in charge of Disruption, the guardian of the temple, the person who has fought more than anyone to nurture Disruption. Some time ago Fiona encapsulated what Disruption is, and is not, writing:

Disruption is:

Being endlessly curious

Keeping an open mind

Looking for new beginnings with larger futures

Anticipating the future without fully expecting it

Accelerating change to your client's advantage

Recognizing patterns of success and building on them

Being creative ahead of the usual agency creative process

Turning intuition into a discipline, but without devaluing intuition

Gaining stability from going somewhere fast

Being in control rather than controlling

Anticipating change rather than defending against it

Questioning the way things are: imagining the way things could be.

Disruption is not:

Change for change's sake

Upsetting the client's organization

A particular creative style

Throwing away the past

Being deliberately wacky

Limited to advertising.

Fiona watches over the constant evolution of our practices and is always trying to improve things. She recently interviewed several of our clients. For me, one of these interviews is especially revealing. It was granted to Fiona by the marketing director of one of the most important banks in South Africa, the SASB (South African Standard Bank), commonly known as the Standard Bank.

The Disruption achieved by this bank lies within its decision to adopt a radically new strategy, grounded in simplicity. Encapsulated in the slogan *Simpler, better, faster*, it represented a 180-degree turn for this long-established financial establishment.

Managing complexity is obviously a skill. This thought was at the very heart of how the Standard Bank saw itself and operated. But the ultimate skill in life consists in making complexity simple. People do not like complications. All they want is their bank to make their life simpler, to save them time. This recognition shook the company's culture. It guided every act, every word. Recruitment forms, for example, began asking this question: "Are you capable of making us simpler, better, faster?" Employees were asked the same question in their annual performance reviews.

Three years later a study conducted by *Global Finance* magazine commended the Standard Bank as being the best in South Africa. It had been transformed by its new strategy.

Here is what Nikki Twomey, head of marketing at the Standard Bank, revealed to Fiona Clancy:

> A clear and strong signal has been given, like a rallying cry. Disruption was the key method getting us there.
>
> We looked at the conventions from the business point of view, the customer's point of view and the marketing point of view. This is where we came to Disruption on some of these issues. It was such a nice case study because we actually did it and it was really successful.

Commenting on a typical Day, Twomey added:

> There comes a moment when you have to act as if you were managing Disney or Microsoft. This moment is always productive. We need to keep these approaches fresh, or people will stop wanting to attend the sessions, we certainly do not want Disruption to become a routine thing. People may ask for a Disruption Day out of laziness. In such cases, I first propose carrying out a classic brand review. We won't carry out a Disruption Day without having seriously thought about it first.

Over the years, our method has gradually evolved, although its fundaments remain the same. When Disruption first appeared at the beginning of the 1990s, the markets were flooded with me-too products. Techniques of major manufacturers had converged so much that we spoke of a "sea of sameness," gradually wiping out all tangible differences between products.

In such a monotonous world, we had to use communication to highlight or even create differences. It was in this era that Philippe Michel, arguably the most prominent advertising person in France, said: "Brands invest millions in their advertising, and they are right to do so. The public is often more captivated by what we invent for them than by what they manufacture. Which has its usefulness: We thank an advertiser for having sponsored a good ad by buying its products."

The market has changed. The business world has embraced new opportunities and adapted to the Internet age. Disruption has found itself faced with a new challenge. After several years in which marketing logic was converging, all of a sudden the old rules have been swept away. Visionary companies have started to create ruptures on every level: business model, products and services, marketing, and communication. Everything can now be questioned, and a company's destiny can be radically changed overnight. Both Apple with the iPod and Sony with its PlayStation proved it possible to move from one market to another with lightning speed, and the likes of Amazon, eBay, and Google have turned our daily lives upside down.

In this turbulent world, the role of Disruption has pivoted. Today it is more about creating a rallying point for a company or brand, a focal point, and this despite the increasing tribulations of the market—or rather, because of them. We need to create a reference point that we can constantly look back to, whatever unexpected directions the market may have taken us in.

Disruption's increasingly radical approach has given rise to a more elaborate and deeper process. In trying to help companies and brands to imagine their future, we have worked on factors of change that go well beyond the simple realms of communication. We have developed new collaborative methods with our clients and forged stronger links with them. Mars is a good example.

Fifteen years have gone by. I am happy that Disruption took off. As I have already mentioned, fifteen thousand of our clients have taken part in Disruption Days. Recently we launched a Disruption Consultancy, which uses Disruption's tools and methods to solve problems that go above and beyond marketing.

One client asked us to organize a Disruption Day to help reconsider how its sales force operated. Another wanted to think about the restructuring of its human resources department. Generally speaking, any time a company is involved in a merger or acquisition process, I believe that there is a role for a Disruption Day.

Every day an e-mail pops up on my computer or a letter lands upon my desk, informing me of a new finding born out of Disruption. Whenever I travel, people in our network express their satisfaction in working for a company with a clear and differentiating culture. And many of those who might leave us end up coming back.

Those who do not return often mention that the company they have joined is looking for something similar to Disruption and that they still have not found anything like it. We have given ourselves a competitive advantage, and we believe it will last.

"You do not have to be the best at what you do. It is better to be doing what others are not," said Thomas Jefferson. We have followed his advice.

* * *

From the very beginning, I held out hope that our defining term, "Disruption," could take on a more positive connotation. I counted on a progressive shift in meaning. Years have gone by, and the tide is beginning to turn, as evidenced in a selection of articles that have appeared in management magazines using the word in a positive sense. Today university professors use the term in their classes.

One of the latest American best-sellers, *Mavericks at Work*, by William C. Taylor and Polly LaBarre, has definitively crossed the barrier, using the word on practically every page, and in a consistently positive sense. Its authors talk of a disruptive business model, a disruptive strategy, a disruptive idea, a disruptive competitor, a disruptive moment, and so on. The crux of the book is that, all things considered, conformists now have no chance of succeeding in business.

A recent article in *Fortune* paying tribute to the staggering success of Steve Jobs ran with the title "Steve Jobs, The Master of Disruption." The shift is happening. In English, the word "disruption" can be positive. It is generating for itself a new sense. Perhaps one day it will even be reborn as part of the French language.

2

The Product

(Or Why Advertising Has to Change in a World of Interactive Dominance)

Disruption was invented at the beginning of the 1990s. Some people would say that ten or fifteen years is too long for this kind of idea to survive. In such a fast-moving world, the concept would be doomed to fade away, its life cycle having come full circle.

I am not so sure.

I do not believe Disruption is limited to any particular period. It evolves in time, with mentalities and with new technologies, but its foundation remains unchanged. When it comes to finding new ideas, it will always be effective to start by questioning Conventions. The principle is unending. It is only what is conventional that changes. Indeed, my first book on Disruption, in 1996, concluded with this phrase: "Today's visions will be tomorrow's conventions."

This chapter and the next one are dedicated to tomorrow. That said, it is always easier to know where you are heading when you know where you are coming from. That is why I propose taking a brief look, just for a few pages, into the past. It will help us better understand where the world of marketing and advertising is going.

So, a quick flashback.

The year 1984 was a milestone. It was the year that saw Apple announce the imminent arrival of the Macintosh with its advertising commercial of the same name: *1984*.

All American advertising people know this film by heart, even though it was only broadcast once . . . I am talking about the film, directly inspired by George Orwell's book, where a woman throws a sledgehammer against the screen with Big Brother's face on it, smashing it into pieces. The crowd rises up to claim its freedom, finally liberated from Big Brother's spell.

Here Big Brother represented man's alienation from the computer and the young woman the birth of Macintosh. Her actions put everything in a new perspective: the way people saw big companies and brands, their relationship with their computer, and above all, their perception of a certain young company called Apple.

At the end of the film, the following message scrolled down the screen: "On January 24th Apple Computer will introduce Macintosh. And you'll see why 1984 won't be like *1984*." The film was stunning, and loved by all for its intelligence. It anticipated the blurring between commercial advertising and entertainment by twenty years. It had all the elements of a real cinema film . . . in sixty seconds. Its director was none other than Ridley Scott.

Created by our agency in Los Angeles, *1984* was voted "Advertising spot of the century" by the American press. To mark its twentieth anniversary, the American magazine *Creativity* published a special edition dedicated to the best campaigns of the last fifty years. When referring to Apple, it explained why the global creative community considered that it marked the beginning of a new advertising era: "The Ridley Scott grand slam took George Orwell's 1984 predictions for a wild bombastic spin to give an uncannily prophetic peek at the new world order to arrive with the dawn of Apple. Perhaps no one knew the true impact of advertising until this spot came along and transformed the Super Bowl from sports event to the premier showcase of 60-second entertainment."

The article went on to reveal that this spot, launched two years before the magazine, could very well be the reason for the magazine itself to exist.

The 1980s were the glory years of advertising, in particular the mythical year that was 1984. It was also in this year that, after a decade of great advertising for Pepsi-Cola, the BBDO agency would create a film that was truly exceptional on all fronts.

We are in 3002. On a visit to planet Earth, an archeologist and his students discover an electric guitar and baseball bat. The professor explains to the students what these strange objects are, while they casually drink their Pepsis. They then uncover a bottle of a sort, covered in dust, which the professor cleans off with a laser. The viewer recognizes it as a Coke bottle. The students ask the professor what this strange object might be. He hesitates before replying, "I have no idea."

The film was a total mix of styles. *Hard sell* and at the same time *soft sell*. It was a scathing example of a comparative demonstration, with Pepsi predicting Coca-Cola's complete demise. It is also a little gem of humor. It won people's hearts, and the Grand Prix at the Cannes international advertising festival.

My partner Lee Clow uses the term "media arts" to describe what we do. We obviously are not in the business of producing art for art's sake and forgetting about business along the way, yet the fact remains that thirty- or sixty-second films like *The Archeologist* or *1984* are masterpieces in the most complete sense of the term.

THE THIRTY-SECOND TV SPOT

I propose we continue this trip back in time, to a time when the thirty-second TV spot ruled: a voyage into creative advertising history. Our journey will conclude with the present day, where this reign is being challenged by the proliferation of media and the maturity of younger audiences. The new generation deciphers each and every facet of advertising, as if it had become immunized against marketing logic.

I have always been intrigued by commercials. The agencies I have managed have produced thousands of them. In a thirty-second spot, which averages fifteen frames, simply changing the order of the first few frames can have a radical effect on its overall impact. This fact forces us to understand that in advertising infinite attention to detail is vital, not optional.

We are constantly working on honing and enriching our skills. But this is not enough to guarantee success. Even the most famous of directors may be able to produce only one good film from two great scripts. The magic is just not there every time. When everything boils down to thirty seconds, talent is not always enough. The unexpected, the unpredictable, are part of the process of film production. This is why, to protect against this, advertising people must immerse themselves in cinema culture, and constantly watch advertising commercials and movies as a way of perfecting their technique, just as the pianist does with his scales. Above all, they need to stay curious. As Renoir said, you can only learn to paint by walking the museums.

And so, since the 1980s, I have collected hundreds of advertising spots. I have analyzed them closely and use them as the basis for a training seminar on television advertising. This seminar lasts two and a half days and is made up of several modules: "Talking Pictures," "Sound as Image's Other Half," "Time and Movement," "The Creative Idea" . . . We talk about editing, framing, lighting. Through presentations and exercises, we examine the advertising idea, and make observations on cinematography. We learn the difference between a campaign idea and a film idea. We study that very particular object that is the thirty-second television spot. We compare the differences in rhythm and editing between an advertising spot and a cinema film. And finally we sit back in admiration at the commercials presented, a selection of the best in the world.

I enjoyed putting together this seminar, choosing extracts from classics such as *On the Waterfront, Passionate Friends*, or *Battleship Potemkin* to illustrate different points. I also used François Truffaut's book *Hitchcock*, which remains a reference today. I was assisted by a producer in our New York office, a champion of the second-by-second shooting board.

This interest I have in the advertising object has made me a sort of "film entomologist." I have written numerous speeches on television advertising and made a large number of presentations on its evolution. I have always been highly interested in English and American advertising, perhaps even more so than some people working in the industry in these two countries themselves.

I was invited to Geneva a few years ago by Procter & Gamble to talk about the history of creative advertising. I started my presentation talking about selling ideas, which are most often the basis of packaged goods advertising. I moved on to the creative leap, which had inspired a book of the same name, and finally to Disruption. I made Disruption the end result of a way of thinking that is entrenched in the P&G doctrine. I asked people to imagine a linear progression, leading from selling ideas to Disruption.

For this to work, of course I had to reinvent history somewhat and revisit some key moments. But the process allowed me to offer an instructive journey into the universe of mass market consumer goods. Above all, I liked the linear aspect of the presentation.

When my friend Jacques Bille, master of business administration director at the Sorbonne, asked me to lead a class on advertising creativity, I opted for the same type of approach. I began with a demonstration produced at the beginning of the 1950s for Band-Aid, and I concluded with observations on the evolution of the thirty-second advertising spot in the Internet age. The audience could feel a kind of linear progression. Of course, in reality, things are always a bit more complicated, but an illusion of continuity facilitates the teaching process.

As we will see, every ten or fifteen years, the dominant style of advertising has evolved through a series of ruptures. We have progressed from demonstrations to selling ideas, coming eventually to a time when we call on viewers' intelligence and feelings. Registers of expression have since multiplied, resulting in today's multiform creativity. This offers an infinite number of paths which can be followed. There is no longer one dominant mode of expression.

A BRIEF HISTORY OF CREATIVITY
IN ADVERTISING

"Telling is not selling," according to the old saying. From the very beginning, advertising people understood that it was not enough to just "tell," that it was much more effective to demonstrate. When I started in this business, Procter & Gamble was one of my clients. In every meeting I attended, the brand manager would ask me the same question: "Have you come up with a good demo?"

Demonstrations have a bad reputation with creative people, and it is easy to see why. By trying to come up with demonstrations at all costs, a great number of brands have presented us with laboriously executed and artificial scenarios. There were some rare exceptions. One of these is the wonderful film for Araldite glue in the sixties, which for me is the ultimate in simplicity.

It is a one-frame film. A hammer that has been broken in half lies on a worktop. A hand moves in to apply a little glue to each half and holds them together for a brief instant. Next to the hammer there is a nail also cut in two. The hand sticks the nail together just as it did for the hammer. Pause. The glued nail is banged into the plank of wood using the hammer. This is one of the most visually simple and therefore effective demonstrations I have ever seen.

Demonstrations like this captivate us, as if by magic, even though they are very real. My enthusiasm may cause some to smile today, but that day at the Sorbonne, I observed the students when they were watching the film, and I can assure you they were mesmerized.

Unfortunately, demonstrations of this caliber cannot be imagined every day. As a mode of expression, demonstrations ran out of steam, and were replaced with films that sought simply to explain product benefits: Band-Aid sticks, Spic & Span does not scratch, Crisco allows for lighter cooking.

As Hamlet, a British brand of mild cigars, showed over a period of twenty years, it is also a benefit to be consoled on the mishaps of daily life. In one spot, a driver is sitting at a carwash with his window open and becomes completely soaked when the rotating brushes start to turn. In another, raindrops start to fall the moment an artist finishes his picture on the sidewalk. In a third, a cowboy hit by an arrow comes face to face with St. Peter, who consults his files before sadly shaking his head.

The protagonist consoles himself in each instance by smoking a cigar, with the campaign slogan emerging across the screen: *Happiness is a mild cigar called Hamlet.*

The athlete selected to light the Olympic torch at the opening of the Games is being watched by a billion people. He raises his arm majestically, bringing the torch closer to the edge. Nothing happens. He tries again. Still nothing. He opens his packet of Hamlets and, in front of the crowd, sits down to savor a cigar.

This campaign went no further than to "put the strategy into pictures." It was literal. This is the key point. The characters in the spots are upset, and so they smoke to relax themselves. It was both simple and linear, with a clear before and after, which took nothing away from both its humor and its verve. But there came a time when advertisers could no longer do what Hamlet had done, provide a simple, literal argument. Agencies had a limited number of promises available to them: a washing powder made washing whiter, a car could be the fastest or safest, a soft drink quenched thirst, and the like. The brands that had been the first to claim these benefits preempted them.

Subsequent brands had to invent new ideas to differentiate themselves. No longer being able to just express their product benefits literally has forced them to go one step further.

A new approach entered the scene. We called this "the selling idea." The selling idea encapsulated the campaign strategy in just one sentence, often expressed in a slogan, but not always. Contrary to the previous examples, the benefit was not formulated in a literal manner. There was a disconnect, rather than a linear construction.

Among the most famous selling ideas from the past are: *Please, don't squeeze the Charmin; Gleem. For those who can't brush after meal; Secret. Strong enough for a man, but made for a woman; Head & Shoulders. You don't have a second chance to make a first impression; Raise your hand if you're Sure.* All of these are from Procter & Gamble.

Most big selling ideas have remained on the air for over ten years. Strong selling ideas have longevity, which is another reason why they add value to brands.

A great example comes from Treets, a brand that only existed in a few countries. The slogan for Treets was: *Melts in your mouth, not in your hand.* The Mars Group, who owned Treets, took the decision to abandon the name in favor of M&Ms, which was much better known internationally. But at the same time, they kept the selling idea. Any such name change normally results in a loss of sales, however small. But not here. The selling idea was stronger than the brand.

Although it may have aged and may seem a little dated today, the selling idea is nevertheless an advertising form that should not be underestimated. Indeed, several of our agency's recent campaigns work on the basis of what we would have called in those distant times a "selling idea": *Never underestimate the power of PlayStation; The cure for the common car*, which relaunched the Nissan Altima. Or on a more humorous note, *Combos. It's what your mom would feed you if your mom were a man.*

Going back in time and across the Atlantic, let us discuss another great British classic. After a long day on their feet, a group of policemen are invited to drink a glass of Heineken beer. They are standing barefoot. A scientist notes their reactions. The policemen's swollen toes are gradually coming back to life and starting to move, proving that *Heineken refreshes the parts other beers can't reach*, as the slogan went. In another spot, a Roman galley is racing at full speed. The rowers on the left are given an average beer, with Heineken served to the rowers on the right. The pace quickens. The right side rows faster than the left, proving that Heineken is more refreshing. The experience ends when the centurion shouts, "We are going round in circles."

Normally, a campaign idea is exhausted after ten or twenty films have been aired, and the campaign reaches the end of its life. It is time to move on to something else. This was far from the case with Heineken, where over forty films were produced in this same campaign. Paradoxically, the campaign became fresher the longer it ran. Each new spot rejuvenated the idea, showing it from a new angle. Each spot amplified the creative leap. The idea was reinforced through each execution.

Back in the mid-1960s, some years after the appearance of the selling ideas but some time before the legendary Hamlet campaign, Bill Bernbach led a creative revolution. He shook up everything overnight, both advertising people's perception of what they were doing and their ways of doing it. He was the first person to understand that the public needed to be spoken to in a different way.

We all remember the campaign he created for Avis. With it, he introduced a new technique that was subsequently adopted and used by numerous agencies, a technique that turned a negative into a positive. In an environment that tended to only admire winners, no one before Bernbach would have thought of boasting about being second. He proclaimed: *We are number 2, so we try harder*. He made this challenger position the linchpin of the campaign, the "reason to believe" that Avis tried harder to beat the number one.

Since this campaign, the battle between Avis and Hertz has become a classic, like those pitting together McDonald's and Burger King, Pepsi and Coca-Cola, or Apple and Microsoft.

Another great campaign that remains in people's minds, perhaps the most famous, is for Volkswagen. Taking the same approach he used with Avis, Bernbach used the apparent shortcomings of the Beetle, as old-fashioned looking as it was small, to make it the height of fashion. As all of us in advertising know, the ads would become classics. The first print ad asked us to *Think small*. Another said: *It's Ugly but It Gets You There* and featured a photo of the clumsy-looking lunar module, while a third was even more disarming. The headline comprised just one word: *Lemon*.

We also remember Volkswagen's first commercials. In one, filmed in black and white, we can make out the contours of a snow plow in the middle of a snowstorm: "Have you never asked yourself how a snow-plow driver gets to the snow-plow?" asks the voice-over. A Volkswagen starts the first time and drives effortlessly through the snowdrift to the plow.

There have been other memorable films for this campaign, one in particular that stands out in the minds of those who are old enough to have been around at the time. A procession of limousines moves along an empty road leading to a cemetery. In the first, sits the widow of the deceased; in the second, his son; in the third, his associates. None of them seems to be really grieving. I cannot resist the pleasure of reproducing here, forty years after it first aired, the voice-over that is a landmark in the history of advertising. It is delivered by the deceased as if he were reading his last will and testament:

> I, Max Willy Stevenie, being of sound mind and body, do hereby bequeath the following: to my wife Rose who spent money like there was no tomorrow, I leave $100 and a calendar. To my sons Rodney and Victor who spent every dime I ever gave them on fancy cars and fast women, I leave $50 in dimes. To my business partner Jules whose only motto was "spend spend spend," I leave "nothing nothing nothing." And to my other friends and relatives who also never learned the value of a dollar, I leave a dollar.

Through a car window we then see the profile of his nephew wiping away a tear. The voice-over continues:

> Finally to my nephew Arnold, who often said a penny saved is a penny earned and who also often said "Gee, Uncle Max, it sure pays to own a Volkswagen," I leave my entire fortune of $500 million.

At the end of the film, as we all know, we discover that the nephew following the long line of limousines is in a Beetle.

I am discussing these old campaigns because what they reveal to us is ageless. Since they first aired, the public has come to understand that advertising can be both intelligent and sensitive. The work of Bill Bernbach has inspired each and every person who has worked in this industry. He has shaped our way of working. Whether he is aware of it or not, from New York to Shanghai, every talented creative person in the world is his spiritual descendant.

THE LADDER

In the past, there have been several such cycles, where popular kinds of expression were adopted by the majority, not aware that these were in fact becoming trends. But things have changed. No client today would ask us to come up with a product demonstration, few marketing managers would know what a selling idea is, and some of Bernbach's ads may now seem somewhat dated . . .

No one communication model is preeminent today. We use every mode of expression imaginable from one brand to another. However, most creative people tend to retreat systematically to a style with which they are familiar and comfortable. For some, this will be playlets, with witty dialogue. For others, something entirely more majestic, brand manifestos of a sort. For others, trendy or far-out films cloaked in corrosive humor . . . Personally, I think it is a mistake for creative people to specialize in a particular style, just as it would be for agencies. You need to be eclectic.

Over ten years ago, I developed a tool intended to move us toward eclecticism, a tool that allows us to look at different ways of expressing ourselves, whether they are closer to that of Procter & Gamble or of Bill Bernbach. Called the "ladder," it is made up of six boxes: top of mind, attribute, benefit, territory, value, and role.

Today, before we start work on a campaign, we ask ourselves: "Where do I want the campaign to express itself, at which level of the ladder?" There is a choice to be made. Do we want to strengthen the top of mind awareness (as in the case of Budweiser with "Bud . . . Budweis . . . Budweiser") or to highlight an attribute (like Avis being number 2), to outline a benefit (like Tide's demonstrations on cleanliness), or promote a territory (like Levi's selling a bit of America to

Europeans)? Do we want to embody a value (such as Nike glorifying beating your personal limits) or to give the brand a role (like the Macintosh *1984* film about liberating man from machine)?

The ladder does not attempt to cover each and every strategic route, even if it does come close. It is meant as a way of organizing our thoughts, of better understanding when it is time to make a creative leap. The leap from one mode to another is always a crucial moment, representing a Disruption in a brand's life. By asking the public to see the brand in a new light, we can refresh, transform, and reinvent it.

This way of differentiating allows an agency to select one approach that is relevant for Apple and another that is right for Head & Shoulders. It is up to the brand to find its style rather than for the agency to impose its own. The choice of mode is driven by the strategy, not the execution. Choosing to preempt a territory, to represent a value, or look for a selling idea, is a strategic, preplanned decision. And so the role of strategy in advertising takes on a new dimension.

Over time, the ladder has become the main tool of our methodology; it is at the heart of Disruption. It authorizes, even promotes, each and every form of expression. The proof is that one of our Parisian agencies recently chose to use a supposedly obsolete mode, the product demonstration, in one of its campaigns.

A man takes a condom from its packet and rolls it on to his finger. He places his finger on an inkpad to take a fingerprint and presses firmly his finger on to a blank sheet of paper. His fingerprint is clearly displayed on the paper, proving how fine the product is. This agency was founded seven years ago. Yet this is probably the best film it has produced so far, and it is just a product demonstration. Things have come full circle.

THE WATERSHED

Readers might question the fact that most of this chapter is dedicated to the advertising film at a time when articles and forums worldwide are predicting the death of the thirty-second television spot.

The answer is simple: For me, advertising films will always be the best vehicles of emotion, as they combine image, sound, and movement. They cannot be beaten when it comes to delivering big brand messages, expressing what the brand stands for in just a few frames. Apple, Adidas, and Pedigree would never be where they are today without TV spots.

I am convinced that film has a long future ahead of it. Of course, it will evolve, in its conception as much as its style, notably because of the omnipresence of interactivity. We are entering a time when the old-fashioned notion of frequency will have less and less relevance. Advertisers will not look anymore for repetition, but rather for immediate impact. This leads me to think that film lengths will often increase, from 30 seconds to 60 seconds, even to 2 or 3 minutes, or longer formats, kinds of "webisodes."

I also think that the Internet will have an unexpected but direct influence on film quality. An increasing number of commercials, almost homemade with extremely low production budgets, are being broadcast online. Film technique has been mastered so that these "minor films" are often of excellent quality. Sometimes their online success even leads advertisers to air them off-line, on our television screens.

In fact, the Internet allows us to experiment more and to measure the results for less. Interactive media, which was expected to mark the demise of the television spot, will actually contribute to assuring its longevity.

The only difference, but a crucial one, is that people will watch only the films they want to see and only when they want to see them.

As we all know, previous evolutions are nothing compared to the changes brought about by the digital realm. In the future, the people we are talking to will have a remote control in hand or a mouse at their fingertips. Up until now, they have been subjected to the constraints of programming and packaged formats. We are gradually moving from one model to another. In the former, the consumer was subjected; now it is the consumer who decides. Power has changed hands.

This is a watershed.

Bill Bernbach and the rare advertising leaders who left their mark on this profession refused to barge uninvited into viewers' living rooms. Their respect for the audience led them to be increasingly creative. They saw creativity as a manifestation of politeness.

They were ahead of their time in this refusal to intrude. The old-school advertising model, which was often voluntarily aggressive, is definitively obsolete. From now on, unannounced intrusions will no longer be possible.

In the long term, this change will prove to be a good thing. Up until now, creativity has been treated as facultative, a simple opportunity. From now on, it will be a vital necessity.

A CONTESTED MODEL

The transition could reveal itself difficult. A great number of people in our industry are worried. They are afraid that these new technologies may condemn a proven model before its successor is fully ready. In *Advertising Age*, Bob Garfield is speaking of "a collapsing old model. Paralyzed marketers. Disenchanted consumers . . ." And he adds "the fragmentation of mass media creates a different sort of cycle: an inexorable death spiral, in which audience fragmentation and ad-avoidance hardware lead to an exodus of advertisers."

TiVo has been the symbol of this, a pioneer in changing our habits, and this in an incredibly short space of time. In September 2000, an executive from our New York office told me a story about a friend who won a TiVo box in a contest. His daughter was only three months old when he had the box installed. This is what he had to say on his daughter's experience:

Sophie doesn't spend much time watching television, never more than an hour per day. When she does watch, she can choose between the latest episodes of several of her favorite shows we have taped for her. So she can watch them whenever she wants in the day. As for us, we can choose which programs we will allow her to see.

She very rarely watches the commercials. We always fast forward through them, or watch programs with no commercial breaks. If she does come across a spot, she is intrigued and asks us to press pause so she can see what it's all about. She has never had a commercial break forced upon her and so she creates her own out of curiosity. But obviously not all that often.

In any case, she is oblivious to program schedules. She has never had the slightest idea at what time her favorite programs are shown. She is lost when she watches television on a set that isn't equipped with TiVo. We have to explain to her each time that the set doesn't work in the same way as ours. Sometimes we simply cut short our explanation and tell her "it's broken."

This story sums up what is in store for advertisers. To develop new kinds of strategies, they must fully understand the context in which they are operating. They know that they are living in a world where TiVo and other techniques will increasingly prevent advertising from imposing its presence. Advertisers must grasp all the consequences of what is happening. It is one thing to create rupture in a stable world; it is quite another to act disruptive in a world that is already in motion.

Some brands succeed in getting through to their audience without having to spend one penny on television advertising. The brands in question are launched differently, most often virally. This is something we achieved for PlayStation as early as 1995. That year, Sony launched its first game console, and our target was Sophie's elder brother. Our agency had suggested launching the product from the bottom up, creating a phenomenon that people could discover for themselves instead of being presented with it directly. The PlayStation campaign began with a word-of-mouth phase.

Strange, cryptic messages evoked the PlayStation on T-shirts, stickers, and, for the first time, on the Internet. Sometimes these messages were completely disconcerting. One of them was a single number: *9–9–95*. It was left up to the public to guess, but this was in fact the officially chosen launch date for the PlayStation. A second message started to circulate. It simply said: *Enos Lives*. Who was Enos? People guessed that Enos was an anagram of Sony and that the brand was getting ready to launch a major new game.

The key message followed with the first campaign slogan. As enigmatic as it was challenging, it read *U R Not e*, with the *e* appearing printed in red. In other words, *You Are Not red-E, or You're not ready*. With this slogan, we were throwing down the gauntlet, both setting a challenge and affirming: We are sure you cannot handle this game. The street did not wait long to give its answer.

We then moved on to a more classic phase using traditional media, which proved anything but "classic." The tactic involved hiding clues in the media landscape. A revolution at the time, the technique was subsequently adopted by a large number of other agencies, once the trend for viral marketing was launched.

The agency placed what we call "Easter eggs" into ads (that is, clues that cannot be spotted unless you specifically go looking for them). They can take the form of tips for improving your gaming strategy, which come to you in a flash by way of subliminal messages during a film. Viewers who have been tipped off by specialist magazines understood that they could read the clues by freeze-framing each image.

In this way, we had organized a brand discovery game in which large numbers of people vied to take part. The contagious nature of the campaign generated such a multiplying media effect that the message reached a greater number of people than just those in front of their TV screens. People shared the clues they had spotted with each other, which fed the inestimable word-of-mouth phenomenon.

People were more than *red-E* when the console finally hit the shelves. Just one year after its disruptive launch, sales figures for the PlayStation were five times higher than those of the Sega Saturn.

THE NEW AUDIENCE

Ten years have gone by—a whole generation in Internet age terms. Today, to imagine the product of tomorrow, we must begin by understanding the new audience, the people we will be addressing in the future.

As I pointed out, the advertising professional is now faced with a progressive reversal of the roles between the advertiser and the audience, between the sender and the receiver. Each and every one of us can become the departure point in a network that will soon number six billion individuals. Today we all have our own blogs. Tomorrow, we will be our own media, our very own television.

We are confronted with a generation which the Ipsos Research Company named the *My Media Generation*. With the convergence of content and a host of interactive and wireless technology at their fingertips, consumers are rapidly demanding that all media be personalized and tailored to their needs, moods, and desires—which explains their voracious appetite for products like PlayStation Portables (PSPs), iPods, playlists, TiVo, Sidekicks, and BlackBerries, and their market success. This new generation's interests are well known to us all: music, Internet, mobile phones, not to mention the infinite potential for combining all three.

It is easy for this target to create a musical experience that accommodates their every mood and occasion. Music can be personalized for online profiles, home pages, ring tones, and podcasts. Opt-in newsletters, Really Simple Syndication (RSS) feeds, and custom start pages now allow this group to self-select and personalize their online experience. Blogs, wikis, and communities like MySpace, TextAmerica, and Friendster encourage them to publish the minutiae of their lives and invite the rest of the world to participate. They consume media, they shape media, and in fact they have actually become media.

This generation has also been referred to as "Me Inc." It is seen as egocentered rather than egocentric. Psychologist Jean Twenge describes members of this generation as self-centered, confident, tolerant, open-minded, but equally cynical, depressed, anxious, and solitary. The crux of her argument is that they have been brought up to reach for the stars, in the quest for success and celebrity, but at a time when it is difficult to get a solid university education, land a good job, and find a decent place to live, even with two salaries. The gap between hope and reality has become bigger, and the sense of unrest with it, which has led this generation to look inward.

This is a group that likes to draw attention to itself. You can find an infinite number of television series and advertising spots on the Internet that have been reenacted, or even remade. Teenagers, American or otherwise, dream of bringing this or that character to life. Films such as those that appear in the campaigns of Combos, Skittles, and Snickers are perfect material for such creativity, as is the Mac versus PC side-by-side campaign. The more trendy or weird a film is, the more it stimulates new versions on the Internet. Some are more or less faithful to the original, others are completely wacky. Competitions are created for new interpretations, where the participants are the ones who distribute the prizes. Each Internet user is potentially a budding star.

Always on is another expression used to describe this generation. It refers to the fact that they are always connected and permanently doing several things at once: telephoning friends, playing networked games on their console, listening to music, updating their blog, while at the same time downloading podcasts.

Whatever we choose to call it, the fact remains that we can no longer construct our messages to this generation in the same way as before. We have left the previously dominant, linear way of communicating in television advertising far behind. Young people's attentions are drawn more toward instant signs than long messages when they click here or there. They are attracted by symbols, icons, visual metaphors, and the good old slogan. The famous American advertising principle—say what you have to say, say it, and say what you've just said—is defunct. We are entering a nonlinear world, a world of instant impressions.

Today's generation is increasingly difficult to surprise. They have seen it all, yet without becoming blasé. And still, what incredible things are happening in our universe! Here are just a few examples, some of them already Internet classics.

You have probably heard of the Australian who bought an island on the Calypso website for $26,000. Real dollars, virtual island. You could not get more ostentatious. Today, over two million people earn more money from the business they do on eBay than from their regular jobs. Nike's electronic billboard in Times Square let shoppers use their cell phones to customize the soccer uniform appearing on the giant screen above them. Viewers can click on a character's outfit in a TV show, and information about the designer and price will pop up while the show plays on. Casting sessions for characters on new TV series are conducted on the Internet, with viewers voting on who should get the role.

A virtual cemetery has been created, allowing Japanese people living abroad to honor their dead. Pets and Tamagotchis can see their spirits commended there too, because the space available is limitless. Bloggers produced a map of Los Angeles showing each of the places visited by Jack Bauer, star of the TV show *24*. This allowed viewers to follow the peregrinations of the antiterrorist hero even more closely, and to monitor the credibility of the distances he covers in 24 hours. This unplanned initiative eventually influenced the way producers approached the fifth season's scripts . . .

We could devote an entire library to the extraordinary opportunities that are opening up to us today, opportunities even the most observant among us could scarcely have predicted ten years ago. The audiovisual landscape is turning inside out and creating a different context, new media forms, and a likely source of new means of expression. Most of these forms are on the verge of existing and will be touched on in the next chapter.

*   *   *

This ferment of ideas, which could give an impression of rising disorder, not to say even chaos, is in sharp contrast with a new possibility: Everything is becoming measurable.

Soon almost all media will become as precisely measurable as online advertising is today. Instead of vague extrapolations from a panel to determine the number of people supposed to be in front of their televisions, advertisers will know exactly how many people watched a show, how many skipped the commercials, and which ones. This information could be tied to demand-sensing models. If a spot proves more effective than anticipated, the agency will be able to alert the client in order to adjust product supply in anticipation of increased consumer demand.

Advertising Age reminded us that, back in the 1950s, John Wanamaker said: "Half the money I spend on advertising is wasted; the trouble is I don't know which half."

This old question may soon be answered.

3

The Media

(Or Why Advertising Is Entering an Era without Barriers)

In today's world, where audiences are fragmenting and media proliferating, we all have the feeling that everything is accelerating. And that even the rate of acceleration is increasing. It is as if no one is able to forecast how fast will be "normal."

I can remember an ad run in 1971 for Kronenbourg beer. Even back then the slogan began with the words: *In a world where everything changes and is speeding up* . . . So this acceleration began longer ago than we think. But it is now manifesting itself in increasingly complicated ways. We are entering a new era of complexity.

Nowadays, everything overlaps and everything interlinks. The Internet is erasing boundaries, and clear definitions no longer hold true. The message and the media become combined, the real and the virtual become intertwined, the tangible feeds on the intangible, and brands transform themselves into media.

Whilst confusing for some, all of this blurring of boundaries will become a source of great opportunity for those advertisers with the clearest foresight.

THE REAL AND THE VIRTUAL

Londoners recently witnessed a scene of extreme violence. A battle between street hoodlums led them to believe that London was not far from becoming the Chicago of the 1930s. Some were frozen on the spot, watching the scene petrified. Others ran away before the police moved in.

It was actually a shoot for a film we had created for a Sony game called *Getaway*. Later on, television viewers were almost as perplexed as the people who witnessed the shoot. Most did not realize it was a staged scene until a policeman addressed the camera to announce that everything that had just happened was an extract from a new video game.

It had all seemed so real. The hoax was then rolled out into other media: a seemingly serious editorial would appear in numerous publications, leading readers to believe that a crime wave was rampaging across the English capital. Only gradually did they realize it was only about a game.

We produced several such films blurring the line between reality and fiction, between the real and the virtual. Viewers smiled when they were duped each and every time. In fact, what really makes the message powerful, even more than the removal of boundaries, is the ability to navigate from one universe to another. Each world enriches its counterpart. And the possibility to move back and forth between the two is limitless.

Convention calls for the real to be real and the virtual to be virtual. Fiction has now become reality, and the opposite is also true.

The most successful PlayStation game launch recently is an example. I should not have revealed that I am referring to a game, as this means I can no longer count upon the surprise factor, or rather the "hoax factor," which is practically second nature in the digital universe. But it remains a very well-known example, one of those that build the legend of the Net each and every day.

In October 2005 Sony PlayStation prepared to launch its new adventure game, *Shadow of the Colossus*. The problem was that adventure games were no longer cutting edge; they had become a dying breed. In addition to this, our client understandably felt it was a niche game, and as such gave us a niche budget. We decided to tap into our targets' online savviness and love of enigmas to generate a boundless real-time conversation. The players became the media vehicles of our campaign. This proved to be the most effective way to compensate for our limited budget.

Hardcore Internet users would discover a video of an Indian journalist making a documentary. A map of India was inserted to allow viewers to place the town of Mahabalipuram, and maps of the markets in this faraway land and documentaries of archeological digs were shown. The voice-over went as follows:

As the people of Tamul Ladu continue to rebuild after last September's devastating hurricane, the ocean has begun to offer more than just destruction and heartbreak. Just a short distance from the discovery of a centuries-old city at Mahabalipuram, archeologists have made another stunning find. Half buried in the sand and stretching a hundred and fifty feet beneath the ocean lies something that may change paleontologists' understanding of prehistoric biology. These are the remains of a skeleton of human form, yet several meters long.

Cut to Eric Belson, the most famous "giantologist" in the world. His mission: to prove that giants exist. Using his blog as the platform for the campaign, we were able to build a vast online mystery that would lead people on a virtual journey around the world in search of giants. Belson's blog was the nerve center of the campaign, where an immense online mystery was created, with the objective being for people to travel the world virtually in search of giants. On screen, we saw Belson giving university lectures, photos of the so-called giant, an Internet site in a language unknown to radio studios, sites being visited by Internet users, and so on.

Of course, none of this was real. We made it all up. Every news report, every photograph, every international phone number. And gamers all over the world responded.

Every time Internet users asked questions on blogs or participated in forums, our team was ready, adapting the campaign in real time to deepen and expand the mystery. Debates were being held all around the globe. More than 25 million people from 110 countries viewed the campaign. An absolute record.

Giantology is now officially listed as an example of viral marketing on Wikipedia, the world's leading online encyclopedia. Our fictitious characters have received e-mails proposing book publishing deals, interview requests, and proposals for jobs as research assistants.

We can see that, with a campaign device such as the one we used for *Shadow of the Colossus*, the marketer's authority remains intact.

Of course, it requires the active participation of the Internet user, but it is the marketer who continues to lead the dance. However, in a parallel movement, the Internet user is progressively taking control over content. A network of consumers who tag, post, and aggregate content depending on their own interests or taste is usurping the publisher's role of mastering content creation, edition, and distribution.

The Internet is the medium that is both the departure and the arrival point of everything. It allows each one of us personally to become the starting point of a network. As a result, the Internet user can take multiple initiatives, beginning with creating a virtual personality to partner his or her real one. The two are not interchangeable; rather they enrich and feed upon each other. The personality we create for ourselves online eventually can have an influence on our behavior in the real world.

To be convinced of this, we only need to immerse ourselves into the strange world of *Second Life*. This site of exchangeable identities, now known as avatars, is a kind of planetary masquerade. Users enter into role-play and experience the feeling of being someone else entirely. The spectacular increase in the number of sites dedicated to virtual reincarnations within the same lifetime would lead us to believe that there is an infinite need for their existence.

The word "avatar" was first employed to refer to each of the reincarnations of the god Vishnu. It became popular as an official term in the digital universe at the beginning of the 1990s. The *Harvard Business Review* described the nonrealistic aspect of today's ambient virtual world when analyzing its commercial potential: "In Second Life, you find services you might expect: virtual clothing and furniture design, event planning, real estate brokering. But the avatar-run businesses also include detective agencies, which keep an eye on virtual infidelity; a notary public, who guarantees the legitimacy of avatar contracts (and offers mediation services if problems arise); and an advertising agency, which designs and places ads for other avatar-operated businesses."

Nike sold virtual shoes that allowed wearers to run faster than other avatars. An iPod store sells virtual recordings downloaded from iTunes, audible only to an avatar through an iPod. The BBC has rented space to host live music, Reuters news service has a full-time reporter named Adam Reuters who covers events as they happen. And it was recently reported that a Chinese language teacher has made over $250,000 in real-world cash by buying and selling virtual land. Governments are discussing whether they should impose property taxes on virtual real estate . . . In other words, the virtual world of Second Life is becoming faced with a reality check.

So, there is real life on the other side of the mirror. The real and the virtual intertwine and penetrate each other.

Five years ago already, several years before the launch of sites like *Second Life*, we created a film for Sony PlayStation that, by no coincidence, was called *Double Life*. The idea was born during discussions organized by the agency between video game enthusiasts and nonplayers. During these meetings, nonplayers tended to mock players, claiming that they "had no life." One player within the group retorted that the sensations he felt when he played made him feel like he was really alive, which was not necessarily the case in his real, mundane life. The nonplayers were astonished to discover the depth of feelings that gaming brought out in him.

This discussion was the inspiration behind our film. People who led normal, everyday lives entered new lives on returning home, lives that were unpredictable, filled with dangerous missions, voyages into unknown universes, and deadly battles.

The film was a series of scenes focusing on characters of all ages and both sexes. Each had a jaggedness about him or her, adding to the slightly disconcerting dimension of the film: an elderly Indian man, a man in a wheelchair, a child filmed extremely close-up in black-and-white, a young woman with a shaved head in a subway corridor, a worryingly skinny youth, a man wearing a tattered mask, a transvestite, and so on.

The scenes roll out in a tight montage. Each character says his piece, reciting it like a litany over a background of operatic music. Each evidently describes his PlayStation experience, but the serious tone of each actor, along with the dramatic atmosphere of the film, brings a certain element of ethos and dignity to their words. Their voices punctuate the successive frames dedicated to each character:

> For years, I've lived a double life.
> In the day, I do my job
> I ride the bus, roll up my sleeves with the hoi polloi.
> But at night, I live a life of exhilaration,
> of missed heartbeats and adrenalin.
> And, if the truth be known, a life of dubious virtue.
> I won't deny it, I've been engaged in violence, even indulged in it.
> I've maimed and killed adversaries and not merely in self-defence.
> I've exhibited disregard for life, limb and property,
> and savored every moment.
> You may not think it, to look at me,
> but I have commanded armies and conquered worlds.

And though in achieving these things I've set morality aside,
I have no regrets.
For though I've led a double life, at least I can say:
I've lived . . .

When this film was launched in 2002, I am afraid I did not really understand its true meaning. For me, *Double Life* was a metaphor, an advertising idea that showcased PlayStation's numerous facets. I had not grasped the fact that it was not a metaphor at all and that, when you lead a double life, the second is just as real as the first.

The intrusion of reality into many virtual worlds is obviously being met with a certain amount of resistance. A large number of Internet users are indeed trying to escape from real life. The boundary can be crossed on the condition that we understand that every virtual world has its own very real culture and that we learn how to work within it. This is how real products will exploit the untapped potential of these virtual universes. The real and the virtual will come together. They will become one.

ADVERTISING AND ENTERTAINMENT

We are living in a complex world where lines are blurring. We even talk about "virtual reality." The real and the virtual are mixed, as we have just seen.

The same can also be said for the boundaries between entertainment and advertising, which are now beginning to intermingle. For some years already, we have been referring to "advertainment."

An episode of the well-known American animated series *South Park* can be used as a good example. Cartman is dropped off in front of a store by his mother, shouting *"I can't wait to see the faces of the others when I show them my PSP. I hope that Kyle's gonna cry."* Noticing the long queue that has formed in front of the store selling the PlayStation console, he shouts out: *"What the hell?"* and marches up to the head of the queue.

Later on, Kenny walks along the middle of the road, playing his PSP. The voice-over informs us that he has reached level 16. Kenny is dancing with glee when a driver, also playing PSP at the wheel, knocks him down. Kenny's soul leaves his body and flies upward. In heaven, a golden PSP is brought over by the hands of an angel. God takes it, saying *"This golden PSP is king of all PSPs."* The angels sing in unison: *"Blessed be the PSP."*

In this case, advertising is no longer an interruption to a program. It is becoming an integral part of it. Taking this evolution still further, we can even envisage advertising becoming a program in its own right.

Campaigns are sometimes so attractive and entertaining that we want to download them. Thanks to a great number of such downloads, more and more commercials are becoming popular beyond their initial reach. This was the case with spots featuring Eminem and U2 for the iPod. When we launched the Irish group's new single "Vertigo," many people asked themselves whether they were watching a television spot or a video clip. The same is true for Spike Jonze's Adidas film, *Hello Tomorrow*, in which the hero moves between the realms of dreams and reality.

When they are not surfing the Net, people spend a great deal of their free time watching series or listening to music. The last spots we produced for iTunes show how a brand like Apple can go beyond its purely commercial function to take on the role of a promoter or talent scout.

To achieve this, we decided to create an entire music experience around a genre. We would begin by choosing a less familiar style of music: jazz. Something people liked but knew little about. We decided to create an original song, and commissioned the legendary trumpet player Wynton Marsalis.

The television spot led people to iTunes where they could download the track and learn more about jazz. Curious music fans would be able to download exclusive live footage we filmed at a Wynton performance and an in-depth interview offering his personal introduction to jazz history, his influences, and his recommendations of other artists, such as Errol Garner or Miles Davis. His music gave a boost to sales of jazz, making it what is now called on the Internet a mega-niche.

Spots such as those featuring the likes of Wynton Marsalis or, later, Eminem, are neither advertising films nor video clips. They represent a new form, lasting forty-five seconds. This mastering of the short format, which advertising does so well, gives even more power and magic to the music. Advertising has now put itself at the service of the artist.

When we talk of Media Arts to define our activities, we are saying that what we are doing is at the crossroads of art and commerce. And this is not a recent occurrence. Twenty years ago, we asked Andy Warhol to design a label for Absolut vodka. *Absolut Warhol* made the brand trendy. Warhol then introduced it into the artistic community. Before long, Keith Haring, Kenny Scharf, Ed Rusha, and a dozen other renowned American artists joined Absolut's circle of friends.

Like any celebrity, Absolut needs occasional publicity boosts to maintain the legend. This has led the brand to pursue new directions, like taking on a role in a film. And not just as an extra.

Throughout the six seasons of *Sex and the City*, its heroines represented the epitome of avant-gardism in terms of fashion, trends, and lifestyles. By using New York and its magnetic locales as the backdrop to each of their adventures, the series' writers succeeded in making *Sex and the City* trendy, avidly followed by millions of viewers around the world.

Trendy, which is exactly what the city of New York and the Absolut brand have in common. This explains why the idea of introducing the bottle into an episode came to life. Rather than settling for simple product placement, Absolut played a leading role as part of the cast. Our agency creative teams met with producers and screenwriters to create an almost tailor-made scenario for the Swedish brand.

In this particular episode, the flamboyant Samantha Jones is trying to launch the acting career of her boyfriend, Jerry. She suggests he pose for an Absolut campaign, inspired by the example of many actors, including Kevin Costner and John Travolta, who made their first appearances in commercials.

Samantha comes up with the title of the poster, *Absolut Hunk*. The photo shows our man sitting suggestively, totally naked, with the bottle of Absolut placed between his legs. The image could be seen as being in poor taste, but for the fact that Jerry is extremely good looking and that photo is merely suggestive. Let us not forget that we are talking here about an episode of *Sex and the City*.

As a public relations priestess with a mightily impressive address book, Samantha wants to use the impact of the campaign to launch her protégé. She prints hundreds of postcards with Jerry's photo and distributes them across New York . . . Meanwhile, the advertising pops up everywhere throughout the city.

Everyone laughs at Jerry at first, and, as he contemplates the huge poster of himself hanging in Times Square, he is persuaded that the campaign will have disastrous effects. The hardly flattering graffiti scribbled about him on various bus shelters only adds to his pessimism. But then, little by little, the situation turns itself around, and he starts being recognized in the street. A cocktail served in trendy bars is baptized Absolut Hunk. The episode closes with him being chased by swarms of teenage girls, screaming "There he is!"

A new cocktail called "Absolut Hunk" was actually created. You can still order it in certain bars in New York. The brand, which held a stately place at the top of the market for over twenty years, was given a new lease of life. The brand took to the street, in Times Square, without sacrificing its chic, classy, and unorthodox side.

This convergence of advertising and programming will continue to take on new forms. In the United Kingdom, for example, we have created for Nissan twenty-four episodes of a television miniseries linked with the TV show 24. Each episode, lasting one minute, is inserted in the twenty-four episodes of the series. The unbearable suspense that Jack Bauer subjects viewers to is repeated in the miniseries that we have created to punctuate the program.

Other brands will want to replicate what Apple, Absolut, and Nissan are doing with us. They will want to share what they undertake with the greatest number of people possible, whether it is in the domain of cinema, music, or sport. Today there is no longer any closed territory.

The opportunity is enormous. But we should also be careful not to underestimate the difficulties involved. Traditional advertising is based on frequency—in other words, the number of times a message is repeated. If it is shown often enough, the message will get through. In a world where brands are part of program content, frequency is losing significance. And so we are forced to invent more interesting content.

We are already used to thinking up numerous ideas for our campaigns, but this is nothing compared to the television industry. Here tens of ideas are considered before just one is broadcast, and even so, there is no guarantee of generating a real, large, and stable audience. The lack of respect we show toward most programs does not mean that we ourselves are necessarily capable of proposing or imagining any better ones.

However, we do have one thing going for us. For years we have been learning to understand our fellow citizens: what motivates them, their way of seeing life and things. We respect consumers, while the television channels tend to give viewers little consideration. It might well be that advertising professionals, these "salesmen," will manage to bring a freshness back to the screen that is sorely lacking today. If so, it would only become yet another paradox.

AWARENESS AND CELEBRITY

What we are about to describe for Adidas is one of the strongest event-led ideas we have ever imagined.

An impressive number of television channels—we have counted over three hundred, from CNN to Fox, from Bloomberg to BBC News—have run features on this event. Scott Levin, journalist for WGRZ-TV Channel 2 News, was quick to voice his surprise. "I don't know how people come up with these ideas," he said when he presented "Sky Soccer." This was the name he gave to the event. We ourselves called it rather more prosaically *Vertical Soccer*.

A reduced-size soccer pitch was created on a huge vertical billboard above the rooftops. Two players challenged each other, hanging from long cords. Defying the laws of gravity, balancing themselves backward and forward, they played a soccer match in midair, secured by bungee cords, alternating penalty, header, overhead kicks . . . all of the moves peculiar to the game. Above the busy areas of Shibuya in Tokyo, and Dontonbori in Osaka, ten-minute matches took place eighty yards from the ground.

People in the street stopped in their tracks, raising their eyes upward to watch these spectacular matches, immortalizing the scene with their cameras or mobile phones. There was such a frenzy that, after a few days, TV presenters and foreign press correspondents got involved in the game. *Vertical Soccer* images soon inundated Japanese, American, German, and English TV screens.

The media wasted no time in picking up the story. In the United States, every major morning show covered the event. Around the world, newspapers such as the *Asahi Shimbun, Nikkei Shimbun, Der Spiegel,* and the *Wall Street Journal* each published articles. One article in particular from the *Journal* summed up the general reaction well: "Once, advertisers hung billboards on humans. In Japan, sports-equipment maker Adidas is hanging humans on billboards . . . The games, held five times each afternoon, bring crowds of pedestrians below to a near standstill. That's precisely the point. In Japan's crammed outdoor-advertising landscape, brands must resort to extremes to grab attention."

In our jargon, *Vertical Soccer* is what we would call an event marketing operation. It is estimated that achieving such coverage would have cost tens of millions of dollars. Any advertiser would be delighted to obtain so much space for almost nothing. Above all, the sight of these two soccer players engaging in football acrobatics was circulated across the entire planet in the space of twenty-four hours. The event accelerated the growth of awareness of the *Impossible Is Nothing* theme. All of a sudden the phrase was known worldwide. It touched on celebrity.

Adidas has engaged in other such initiatives since. The following year, eighty professional climbers went up against each other in impossible sprints up the walls of buildings in Hong Kong and Japan. In 2006, when the official World Cup ball was launched, Adidas offered passersby the opportunity for some real-life action. Sitting inside a giant ball, people found themselves catapulted into the air at a speed of over 100 miles per hour.

At the same time, the brand launched *+10,* a campaign that put the team back at the heart of things. The films showed imaginary soccer games between a young boy, José, and his friend. As in a school playground, the two young captains went to choose the ten players who would make up their respective teams, except that these players were the most famous stars of today and yesterday. Players called David Beckham, Michel Platini, Zinedine Zidane, Oliver Kahn, and Franz Beckenbauer.

Adidas manifests itself in a thousand different ways: classic advertising, sponsoring, events, Internet, and so on. Our job is about managing all of these types of communication and integrating them. The trap to avoid is providing slick campaigns where each discipline and each channel simply translates the central idea without contributing further to it, where mere consistency takes precedence over inspiration. We need to introduce powerful moments into all aspects of our communication plans, as in *Vertical Soccer* or Absolut *Sex and the City*.

People no longer notice what they know too well. This can be described as an excess of familiarity, which ends up making us blind to the ads we have seen too often. The ideas I have just described are designed to avoid the negative effects of familiarity. They put the spotlight firmly on the brand, allowing us to see it more distinctly. The brand creates excitement, just like the Hollywood stars of yesteryear, who certainly knew how to create a helpful scandal from time to time.

The *1984* launch film for the Macintosh became famous literally overnight. A few weeks of word-of-mouth and viral marketing on the Internet were enough to launch the first PlayStation. A repetition of events gave Adidas's communication an instantly global dimension. For three months, Absolut *Sex and the City* became a lively topic of conversation in the bars on Second Avenue.

Each time we went above and beyond the traditional role of advertising. We did not stop at building awareness; we strove to create celebrity. We wanted the campaign to become world famous, leading the brand to become so in turn.

THE IDEA BEHIND THE IDEA

Our job consists in optimizing each touch point between a brand and its public. Today we can animate digital billboards at busy traffic circles; create communities of bloggers on the Internet; encourage the public itself to create slogans, clips, and music to promote a brand; erect giant posters on building fronts; set up microsites on mobile telephones; and so on. The list is endless.

One of our media executives in Los Angeles has established a list of over one hundred such touch points. The time when the choice was merely among television, poster, or print seems a distant memory. We can choose tens of different touch points and animate their interaction in a thousand different ways. The palette of opportunities is growing in an exponential fashion.

From now on we will be dealing with three key factors: ideas, their chronology, and their interaction. Action plans are now becoming orchestration plans.

What kinds of ideas are we are talking about? I have distinguished between different sorts of ideas and have even suggested the formulation of another "ladder," one that starts from strategic ideas on one hand and would extend to execution-led examples on the other. Obviously any such classification is risky, and there will always be an idea that escapes fitting onto a predetermined rung. But the initiative is nevertheless useful, since it makes it easier to understand each other when discussing these ideas.

The first kind of ideas are big brand ideas, such as *Think Different, Shift*, or *Impossible Is Nothing*. Each is as profound as it is big. Profound because each gives even more meaning to the brand it represents, big because each can be easily expressed through all channels. These are welcoming ideas that embrace all media and bring together multiple executional ideas, as in the case of *Vertical Soccer*. Is this Adidas initiative a poster, a sporting event, or a public relations campaign? Whichever definition you choose to give it, the initiative increases the strength of the *Impossible Is Nothing* idea tenfold.

At the other end of the spectrum we find precisely what we call executional ideas. In practice, it may happen that we come up with some such ideas even before we have defined a strong brand idea.

A few years ago our Swedish agency organized a soccer tourna-ment for SBAB, an outsider in the banking market. SBAB invited the three largest banks in the country to meet them on the pitch, as a way of showing that a small outsider is not afraid to challenge well-established institutions. The chairman of SBAB went live on television to invite the directors of these large banks to the competition. The event cre-ated a buzz that was picked up by every television channel around.

The match eventually took place at the National Stadium. SBAB lost 5 to 1, but sales of home loans increased by 220 percent. Up until that point, this event had only been a strange idea to get a new com-pany talked about. Challenging leaders, more or less aggressively, has always been an outsider strategy. But what next? The soccer match idea seemingly had no future. As it was in no way linked to a larger brand idea, it appeared to be a simple one-shot stunt.

The following year, a new idea was launched. Human billboards paraded on the sidewalks outside competing branches, wearing mes-sages proclaiming SBAB's advantageous interest rates. Bank managers rushed out of their offices to try to get rid of the human billboards. Unfortunately for the bank managers, every moment was filmed, and the footage was broadcast shortly afterwards.

The human billboards proved something to us that we had not understood with the soccer match. The SBAB campaign was indeed a classic challenger campaign, but with one important distinguishing feature: The challenge took place in real life. It never took the form of a story told in the imaginary world of television advertising. It was just real.

We called this campaign *Street Challenge*. One word can change everything. It can make the past clearer and open up the door to future horizons. In this case, that word was "Street." In the years that followed, other ideas ensued, always taking place in the street. For example, a new product was invented and named "the Loan in a Can." Thousands of cans, each containing a loan offer, were stacked on supermarket shelves and in street corner kiosks.

The following year housing loans were delivered like pizzas. You only had to dial a number, and a real housing loans advisor got on his scooter to come to see you. Initiatives of this kind continued to attract a record number of visitors to the SBAB website.

The creative teams at our Swedish agency had thought it was time to change the rules of the game, that advertising was no longer enough, and that they should come up with tangible ideas, like the soccer tournament, and then introduce the advertising inspired from those ideas into the real world. In their words: "We need to come up with something else rather than advertising, and advertising must be the consequence of that something else." By working like this, advertising impact is increased immeasurably.

While we organize Disruption Days with our clients, we organize Connection Days between ourselves. Each and every discipline specialist is brought together around one table. We do not come up with a new brand idea every time, but very often participants will come up with new types of ideas, like the soccer match, ideas that are most often linked to their main discipline.

Somebody from an events company will bring an event idea to the table, the person from the direct marketing agency a loyalty idea, and so on. We retain the best ideas. But more important, we ask ourselves if one of them hides a bigger idea, a brand idea. *Street Challenge* was a brand idea lying hidden in SBAB's human billboards. We have created a tool to detect these big ideas, and its name encapsulates its objective. We call it "the Idea behind the Idea."

One thing will remain forever: Ideas make the difference, whether they are big brand ideas or smaller but nevertheless vital ideas, such as Absolut *Sex in the City* or *Vertical Soccer*. The second feed the first by giving them wider reach. They extend their life span.

The practices of the profession are being transformed from top to bottom. My generation satisfied itself with finding ideas. The next will also have to invent the channels to go with them. For the Generation Internet, the idea and the media are one and the same, and media immersion and a perfect understanding of channels and audiences will be a source of inspiration. Here again the "after" will influence the "before." The channel will inspire the idea.

TANGIBLE AND INTANGIBLE

Real, virtual . . . Tangible, intangible . . . These notions, referring to seemingly opposite worlds that in fact are not separate at all, have always intrigued me. Over ten years ago now I wrote about "tangibles" in advertising. I talked about those campaigns that, like SBAB, were based on something real. The example of *Fresh TV*, a campaign from Goodby Silverstein, is the one I referred to most often.

Chevys is a chain of Mexican restaurants that aired advertising spots the same day they were filmed. These films were only shown one evening. In the first frame of every film, the words *Fresh TV* appeared in bold letters. It is hard to imagine a more tangible idea than throwing away films only a few hours after they have been produced. It symbolizes Chevys' intransigence regarding the freshness of the products it serves up.

This intrusion of reality into the sterile world of television screens creates a shock. *Fresh TV* sticks in our minds after just one viewing. If advertising people were not so quick to forget that impact is the sine qua non condition for success, they would look for solutions of this kind more often. They would look for these tangible ideas that shake up the intangible world.

Two of the best-known journalists in Turkey are husband and wife in real life. The husband, a highly regarded commentator, became the spokesperson for a diaper brand in an advertising spot. He smiles broadly, whispering to the camera that these diapers are so extraordinary that they could persuade women, like his own wife, to have children. The journalist then asks his wife to think about it. The camera cuts to her in the background, a seemingly surprised look on her face. A series of spots follow with the husband continuing to use the pretext of the product in an attempt to convince his wife to start a family.

Several months later, the celebrity press announced that she had just given birth. Her husband's strategy had worked, it seemed, and she had finally come round to the idea. In reality, our agency creative director was a friend of the couple and knew full well that she was already pregnant, which gave him the inspiration for this stunt. The campaign had an even greater impact than we could have dreamed of.

The French Railways antifraud campaign is another example of a tangible idea, although one based on a hoax. The agency painted false escalators, false rest room doors, false information screens, and false luggage trolleys on the walls of train stations. It was a very effective optical illusion. People thought they were real. The moment the traveler realized that the door handle did not exist, he would find a small poster stuck to the middle of the false door that read: "Without fraud this door would really exist. Fraud costs us two hundred million dollars every year. To fight it, the SNCF is taking a number of measures in all stations and trains." For the first time, the campaign created public support for an effort which had not always been received positively, the SNCF's attempts to crackdown on fraud. This helped reduce the number of nonpaying passengers by 17 percent the first year.

These tangible ideas give more substance to the intangible, in other words, to advertising. We can distinguish between different kinds of such ideas. There are those advertisements designed just to create impact, like the SNCF optical illusion. These intriguing ideas immediately raise interest and often get amplified through extensive media coverage. And there are the other kinds of ideas, those that are more engaging, that immediately give more weight to the brand promise. We cannot imagine that a company throwing away its advertising film every night, as it is no longer fresh, will propose anything less than the freshest of foods.

This leads me to the following observation: Today, we no longer judge brands simply by the products they make or the services that they propose, but by the way they behave. Brands need to know how to take initiatives . . . and how to reinvent themselves. The time has come when words need to become action.

As I have mentioned, we have been working with the Pedigree brand for a few years now. What better way to prove this company's love of dogs than to launch a wide-scale campaign to encourage adoption? This became the *Pedigree Adoption Drive* program.

Several short films were broadcast, each time with a different dog shown behind bars. The slogan *Help us! Help dogs!* was written across the final frame along with a telephone number. The voice-over said: "This is Max, one of thousands of dogs looking for a home. Every time you buy a can of Pedigree, we make a donation so that abandoned dogs can find a home."

Several concrete actions were taken at the same time, most often in collaboration with centers for abandoned dogs. The results were spectacular. Several thousand dogs were adopted thanks to the operation, and nearly $2 million was donated to the shelters. In this respect, results went beyond expectations. Whilst at the same time, Wal-Mart sold more Pedigree dog food than in any other period in its history.

Danone's healthy living initiatives are another example of what a brand can do when it practices what it preaches. Since 1991, when we recommended the creation of a health institute, Danone in France has become the acknowledged intermediary between the universes of health and food.

The institute is made up of scientists, doctors, and researchers whose mission is to widen our knowledge of the consequences that food choices have on our health. Studies have been conducted on teenage eating habits, anorexia, prenatal nutrition, obesity, and the immune system.

The spots that were broadcast were based on the idea of Hippocrates, that what we eat is our first form of medicine. One of them brought together a child, his father, his grandfather, and his great-grandfather. The voice-over explained:

> Today we can expect to live twenty years longer than a century ago. The progress made in terms of our nutrition has been a contributing factor. Thanks to research, tomorrow food could become our first form of medicine. We will have a better chance of noticing that this little fellow looks like his great-grandfather. Every year the Danone Institute encourages young researchers in their work on nutrition.

Showing that a child could know not only his grandfather but also his great-grandfather was a moving way of expressing the benefit of long life expectancy. Moving and highly effective.

A large number of companies—Danone is just as relevant an example as McDonald's or the SNCF—have created such types of action programs. They are not just satisfied with selling their products and promoting their brands, they also take action. And we judge them on how they act.

In this way, we could talk about "brand programs." The word "program" actually has an interesting double meaning. On one hand, it describes a set of actions, the commitments of a political party, an association, or, in this case, a brand. On the other, we can use the term to describe the diverse elements of a show, whether it is a piece of theater, a concert, or television. And so when we say that brands are going to start proposing programs, we understand what is happening in both senses of the term.

Adopting dogs, reducing fraud, fighting for better nutrition: It is clear that brands are quite capable of introducing programs that are oriented toward topics of general interest. When they succeed, they become intermediaries between people who love dogs and the strays up for adoption, between people who respect the SNCF rules and those who do not, between the mothers of young children and nutritional experts. They contribute to both the tightening and the strengthening of today's social fabric.

And so brands become media, in the original sense of the term.

This convergence between brand and media deserves clarification: Long gone are the days when a company would get involved with the media only in the strict marketing sense of the term, as a vehicle for its commercial message. Today the brand goes beyond developing promises that satisfy existing needs. Today it produces an entire cultural package, it brings aspirations to life, and it is concerned with public, not just commercial, issues. Brands take the high ground and raise the level of the debate. It has therefore become legitimate to analyze brands with the same critical eye as, for example, a press publication.

When Danone reports on its research into the link between food and health and publishes information of an editorial nature, we have the right to expect a higher level of rigor, or ethics, in what they do.

However, one fact appears to go against this seductive "brand-media" formula. The brand supposedly does not possess any of the three characteristics we consider to constitute a media.

What makes media media is the effect of associating a specific platform (printing paper, the air waves, the DVD disc) with a protocol (writing, a fixed or mobile image, sound, voice) and a method of distribution (sales, subscriptions, broadcasting, online communication). Therefore brands could not be described as media in the strictest sense of the term . . .

This being said, these last few years have seen the development of new forms of communicating that blur this distinction. New technologies are allowing brands to enter into direct contact with their audiences, and brands also are using their "proprietary" media increasingly skillfully, in addition to the media they purchase. The retail store can become a studio or an event in its own, the brochure can become a magazine, and the television spot can be perceived as a program in its own right.

Furthermore, a new era has arrived with broadband Internet, which allows brands to transform their Internet site into web TV. QuikSilver TV is competing with MTV, FCUK radio competes with popular music stations in the United Kingdom, and perhaps tomorrow Wal-Mart TV will challenge CBS by offering "life, real life," seven days a week, 24 hours a day on our screens.

If brands can extend to become media in their own right, it is also because the primary definition of media itself is transforming before our very eyes.

Traditional mass media communicates the same cultural content to a general group of people through a fixed device associating a platform and a protocol. New media, and the Internet in particular, are free of these two limitations. New ways of delivering content in all kinds of formats are freeing even the most traditional forms of media, such as the press, from the rigid association between platform and protocol. This change encourages the emergence of media with multiple platforms and targets whose unity relies only on a corporate name, such as *The New York Times* or Danone. On these playing fields, the brand can now compete with the medium. In a way, the brand actually becomes a new medium, by making its mark on a set of aspirations that flow through today's society.

*   *   *

When discussing the numerous institutional initiatives taken by McDonald's, from cooperating with the agricultural industry, to launching new kinds of recruitment and training schemes, Larry Light, former global marketing director of the Chicago-based company, did not hesitate to refer to "brand journalism." While we might refer to brand media, to many the combination of the words "brand" and "journalism" will be inappropriate.

Light simply wanted to point out the end of monolithic marketing and one-way communication. Until now, every brand had to communicate one message, and only one message. That time is over. From now on, brands must communicate on all the initiatives they undertake, like an endless chronicle.

To help these initiatives find their public, brands now have within their reach an entire range of multiple, complex, and entangled channels and platforms. The strongest ideas will result from managing this interaction, which is born of the blending of the real with the virtual, of the commercial with the editorial, of the tangible with the intangible, of the factual with the imaginary, and of the artistic with the scientific.

The world of communication has never been so wide open.

4

The Agency

(Or Why the Agency of the Future Will Be a Place of Cultural Blending)

The level of competence within the same profession can vary enormously. Consider doctors, lawyers, and architects. They are far from being equal.

The same also holds true for us advertising people and our agencies.

In addition, we share with architects the fact that our work is on display in the public arena, unprotected from the scrutiny of public opinion, an opinion that quite rightly rises up against the mediocrity and poor taste of a great number of commercials and posters.

The residual effect of this mediocrity may well be short-lived, but it contributes to creating an unflattering image of our business. I see disappointment in the eyes of those around me when I tell them what I do for a living. I need to elaborate quickly. Their attitudes change when I add that our agency is responsible for campaigns for Apple, Adidas, and Sony. The conversation starts to flow, and I am bombarded by questions about this or that campaign. People ask me for prints of our latest work. All of a sudden I belong to an almost enchanted world, where the most surprising of powerful, colorful images move to the beat of the week's most popular music.

Our profession lies at a crossroads between art and business. We craft language that is intended to be effective but that, at the same time, can make people smile and sometimes even move them. We count the most diverse collection of talents, from highly specialized anthropologists to fashionable film directors. Succeeding in our business requires a unique agility, being able to move rapidly from the shrouded world of banking to the high-paced world of computers, from the light industry of dairy products to the heavy industry of the automobile. We build brands with their own forms of expression, which, when we breathe life into them, breathe life in turn into our clients' businesses.

We live the vibrations and pulsations of the free market economy, convinced from the inside that it is the only kind of economy with a future. We fight our daily battles, punctuated by the fiercest of new business pitches. These are more often lost than won, since in new business there can only ever be one winner. We are the practitioners of a minor art form that a hundred years from now will be one of the most accurate reflections of our time. So why not leave the most beautiful traces that we can? We invent ideas to simplify complex problems. We wake up every morning hoping to get excited about the next new idea. And often we succeed.

Aldo Papone has been senior vice president of American Express, The Body Shop, and Macy's. He was kind enough to endorse my first book on Disruption. Over the last thirty years, he has selected advertising agencies and consultants all over the world. Here are his words on our profession:

> To commission a thorough and accurate analysis of your company's market from a management consultancy—its strength and its weaknesses, its competitors and its future—is always worth doing. But as management, you are still left wondering what to do with all this information.
>
> The wonderful thing about a good agency is that the analysis can be just as thorough, but they also leave you with actual things: practical recommendations—words, pictures, design, programs—that you can actually do something with.

And he adds, surprised: "I often wonder why we don't make more of that." It is a good question. I believe clients need their agencies more now than ever, for a lot of reasons.

Only agencies know how to bring a brand's meaning to the surface, how to communicate a brand's soul. We are experts at distilling a thought into a few words.

Only agencies can deliver the kind of integrated communication today's clients expect. Because integration is not a science, it is an art, and we are the only real orchestra conductors available.

Only agencies can rebuild the bridge between media and creative. To get better discounts, clients have encouraged the rise of media companies, leading to a division between media and the creative world. This has proved to be the wrong trade-off. What clients have saved in cost, they have lost in intelligence, or rather that part of intelligence that used to exist between media and the creative realm.

Only advertising agencies can provide strategic advice together with creative solutions. Our clients are tired of spending fortunes on consultants who can only report what is already there. Dry analyses of mere facts are not very helpful. Agencies know that the future of brands cannot be predicted, only imagined.

It has taken time, but some clients are finally beginning to understand the great value that agencies can provide. No other entity is capable of delivering all these benefits. And even more importantly, all at the same time, which is vital, since today all these activities are interconnected.

TRANSVERSALITY

Charles Handy, the essayist and author of *The Age of Unreason* (1996), wrote that many companies would do well to follow the advertising agency organizational model. Advertising agencies operate transversally, with people from a number of different disciplines—commercial, creation, finance, planning, media, production—constantly crossing boundaries.

Everybody works together on a project basis, without hierarchy. The specialized departments in agencies like ours are made up of forty to fifty people. The people from these different groups are assigned to brands for a long period. This leads to the formation of teams that are dedicated to servicing each specific brand, such as Adidas, Nissan, and Danone.

One of Carlos Ghosn's great contributions at Nissan has been the successful breaking down of silos between departments and countries. For each major issue to be resolved, Ghosn created "cross-functional teams," each made up of around fifteen people from different nationalities and disciplines.

Working like this comes naturally to us. Something that is very difficult to achieve in a large industrial company is much easier in a service company on a smaller scale. An art director, often with a degree in graphic arts, perhaps someone who is an exceptional craftsman without necessarily being very well read, can work side by side with a strategic planner with a PhD in semantics. This is what I love about this business. It is so inspiring to see people coming up with strong ideas for the very reason that they come from such different horizons.

Agencies are melting pots. People from all origins and disciplines work together in an orchestrated fashion, each benefiting from one another's work. To achieve this harmonious interaction, it is crucial that there is no dominant element in the group and that no discipline is considered more important than another. This is an essential condition to enable transversal thinking, in other words, the blending of the minds and skills of one discipline with another.

BLENDING SKILLS

Obviously, managing a large global company is not an easy task. But a first step toward success is to start by identifying what you are doing right. When a company is operating in over one hundred countries, it is statistically impossible that intelligent initiatives have not been taken here or there. You only need a little curiosity to uncover them, but you need real curiosity, something that appears difficult for many companies.

Some, however, are very good at encouraging the ability to observe, developing what one American author has called "the art of enthusiastic imitation." The eternal not-invented-here syndrome is declining in these companies. And it is in this kind of environment that people learn the most.

These organizations know that there is a real untapped growth potential lying in the identification of best practices. The term may be a little worn out. But Procter & Gamble, once again, owes its success to exploiting best practices: Its employees search for what really works, then invest all the time it takes to deeply understand the reasons for this success. Once this knowledge has been gained, and only then, P&G systematically implements the new practice throughout the world, and with phenomenal speed. A. G. Lafley, Procter & Gamble's chief executive officer, says that it is the speed with which best practices are rolled out that gives his company its competitive edge.

For our part, we are multiplying the sources of information on our most successful experiences. We have created a Disruption Bank that includes over a hundred filmed case studies. We have developed think tanks, which we refer to as *rings*, each made up of around twenty employees from across the world. There is a Disruption ring, a planning ring, a public relations ring, and so on.

We also organize top-level training seminars. One of them, held over the course of five days, is called "Learning for Leaders." Others are of a more practical nature. Our "how-to" programs give tips, tactics, and techniques to provide our people with a road map to faster growth, which results in a melting pot of skills. Each of us is enriched by the expertise of the ten thousand other employees who constitute our network.

There is no denying the progress we have made in the last five years. But despite these efforts, we still have a long way to go. I often realize how difficult it is to circulate information, to cascade down the knowledge. I am always reminded of Lewis Platt, the former chairman of Hewlett Packard, who once said: "If Hewlett Packard knew what Hewlett Packard knows, we would be three times more profitable."

BLENDING DISCIPLINES

We advised Danone to create a health institute. We have been invited to discussions on Apple's packaging and on the interior design of the Apple Stores. We recommended that the leading Swedish Internet bank create a new type of property loan. We propose new product ideas to Pedigree. We help launch a new PlayStation game online every week. Through all this, we are involved in each of the myriad ways brands interact with their audiences.

We refer to "touch points" to describe the different ways a brand enters into contact with its audiences. These touch points are points of contact that can go through several channels and take numerous different forms. Often a far cry from the sacrosanct thirty-second television spot, these touch points are conceived by specialists from many disciplines, from interactive to direct marketing, from event management to sales promotion, and others.

What is crucial is to make everyone want to work together. Certain communication groups claim they are experts at this, and talk about multimedia, integrated communication, holistic communication, and media neutrality—"neutral in terms of media choice," that is. They refer to "connection planning," where the agency's role is to optimize each contact point and manage them in time and space, as well as ensuring their interaction.

Now that all agencies present themselves as multidisciplinary groups, connection planning has become the Holy Grail. These agencies act as if they have only just discovered that every point of contact matters, as if they had uncovered something new. The largest communication networks all want to make connection planning their point of differentiation. But it is not the mere existence of such a discipline that will make the difference, but rather the expertise that is built up over time. We are all engaged in the same race; no one has opted out. The winners will be determined by the actions they take, not the postures they make.

This new way of working stems from an obvious fact that has been largely ignored over the last twenty years: that we should be talking about audiences. And not "targets." Audiences are composed of people who are interested in brands, and they also happen to be the ones who *consume* media. They are of course the same people. This fact renders essential the merger of strategic and media planning, of brand and audience specialists.

The word "connection" is as abrupt and cold as it is uninspiring. Moreover, it simply describes a means to an end. As I have already mentioned, Lee Clow prefers the term "media arts." He says: "We are in the media arts business, we are not an advertising agency, unless advertising is being totally redefined by the totality of communication arts that are at our disposal. Store design, such as the likes of the Apple Store, as well as packaging and products design, like that created for Pedigree, are part of advertising."

When we refer to "the arts," we are of course talking about applied arts, living arts. But it only takes one visit to an Apple Store to see that the designing architect must be a very talented artist.

We are becoming communication artists who use the media to connect with people and invite them into the universes we are creating for the brands we work for. Each time consumers come into contact with the brand, they judge it. This is why everything that we undertake for a brand must be thoughtful and inspired. Everything must be creative, since each point of contact with the brand can determine its relationship with the consumer.

We can no longer permit a lack of connection between what appears on the Internet, on television, in the store, and on the packaging. A brilliant campaign should not have to support a product with poor packaging. Yet, for years, agencies stayed in the comfort of their own space and did not get involved.

We must not let go. Everything counts. There are dozens of possible touch points between a brand and its customers. Each of these touch points must be true to the idea of the brand and increase its differentiation.

We have set up a Media Arts Lab, a sort of laboratory in which we seek to fine-tune our understanding of how communication will work tomorrow. Situated in Los Angeles, across the road from our agency, it shares the same offices as Frank Gehry. We are convinced that the future of our profession lies in the blending of design with interactive technologies. All the people working on the Apple account are part of the laboratory. They work on the relationship between advertising, design, interactive marketing, and entertainment. They are lucky to have Steve Jobs as a client, Frank Gehry as a neighbor, and Hollywood as their environment. It is the ultimate mix, and the lab is shaping our methods of tomorrow.

Often the most unexpected ideas emerge when creative people from different universes work together. Cultural collisions should be encouraged. Having said that, it is not enough simply to bring together specialists from different horizons. There must be a clear sense of direction. It is the role of our strategic tool, Disruption, to provide this direction. If everything is based on a strong central idea, usually a brand idea, then it is easier to express it in every way and shape imaginable. And this is the function of media arts. This is how Disruption and Media Arts inspire one another.

We are not alone. Increasingly, we need to call on outside talents to contribute to specific projects, at specific times. This might be an anthropologist, a graphic designer, a sociologist, a nutritionist, a screenwriter, an architect, a graffiti specialist, a statistician, a semiologist . . . The list of specialized talents is long. Procter & Gamble is already creating over half of its new products with the help of outside experts. Most often this creative process involves very small structures, consultants, and even people working on their own. The corporate world feeds on free-thinking individual initiatives.

While most organizations choose to capitalize on what they already know, companies that are really creative make a concerted effort to allow thinking from the outside world to infiltrate them. Advertising agencies need to do the same and be on the constant hunt for new intersections, unexpected collisions. In the words of Alex Graham, one of the best-known television producers in the United Kingdom: "What is so great about this business is that you start out with a blank sheet, asking yourself who you want to work with rather than who is available."

BLENDING EMPLOYEES

One of the most critical things in our business is also the most difficult to transmit. You are either born with it, or you are not. What I am talking about is this taste for diversity, the exhilarating feeling we get from discovering new cultures, creative approaches from other parts of the world, behaviors that we do not always understand at first.

In India, members of the Brahmin caste do not work. Therefore, presumably no one in our industry comes from this caste. No one, that is, except Sandip Mahapatra. When asked to justify himself, he was quick to explain: "I am a planning director. My job is to think, not work." I have remembered this, along with a number of other anecdotes that I hold dear, from the more lighthearted of retorts like Sandip's to those of a more serious nature, each furthering my understanding of the differences that, due to their cultural nature, go much deeper than we could ever imagine.

I have visited Tokyo many times since the Renault-Nissan Alliance took place in 1999. Robert LePlae, head of the Nissan account at the time, and I have worked closely with Hakuhodo, Nissan's agency in Japan, an institution ranked second in the local market. In June 2006 we carried out the merger of Hakuhodo's Nissan division with our Tokyo agency. I know several of the agency's executives on a personal level and have forged solid friendships with many of them. One day, tired by a seemingly never-ending discussion, I asked a simple question: "Is this a disagreement or a misunderstanding?" Perhaps it was indeed a disagreement, but their politeness, or desire to move forward, made them decide it was just a misunderstanding. I have asked this question several times since then, and it generally puts an end to all arguments.

Years have gone by. Both companies, Hakuhodo and TBWA, have invested a lot in trying to understand each other better. The end result is, I believe, a level of trust rarely achieved between a Japanese and a Western company, a trust that has been built slowly, step by step, meticulously.

We gain inspiration from cultural exchanges. As I mentioned, we have created multiple rings, think tanks that bring together staff from all over the world in real time, as well as exchange programs for both the most novice and the most experienced of our people. We have also set up creative commando groups, founded on the principle that when faced with a difficult problem, it is more effective to encourage creative people of all nationalities to work together. Note: together, not side by side.

This initiative is a direct response to a question we were asked several years ago by Steve Wilhite, at the time marketing director of Nissan in the United States. Steve was surprised that we were not taking advantage of the creative capabilities of our agencies outside of America—those in South Africa and Australia, for example. Steve was right. Although we were asking agencies from various countries to work together on our global campaigns, the campaigns that Steve was responsible for were exclusively aimed at the American market, and only creative people from our American agencies were working for him.

Overnight, we created "creative commandos," which we called SWAT teams. When a difficult problem arises, we elect three or four teams from different countries to spend a week or two together. Recently American, Slovenian, Chinese, and German teams shut themselves away for a week in Hamburg to work intensely together. Though creative people are sometimes accused of being individualist and lacking in team spirit, I can confirm that the enthusiasm on these teams is so strong that we had to set up a waiting list for future SWATs. Creative people from across the entire world want to be part of our next commando unit.

The Chinese who worked with the Slovenians continue their relationship on the Internet. There is nothing to stop the solution to a problem raised in Shanghai coming from Ljubljana, and this without the client or the head of our Shanghai agency even being aware of it.

In the final analysis, it is the attitude of each individual that really matters. Either you really enjoy trying to understand the thinking behind a disconcerting campaign presented to you by a Korean art director or you just do not care. An advertising network resembles the United Nations on a smaller scale, but a United Nations that works. Our differences are no obstacle to us. On the contrary, they help us to grow.

FROM ONE WORLD TO ANOTHER

In working in New York, I myself am a part of this blending.

When I return to Paris, I am often asked how I feel to be a Frenchman at the helm of an American network. It is a question that I have never been asked by people in America; perhaps that indicates that what is surprising in Paris is normal in the United States.

Nobody in the TBWA network ever asks me about my origins. It is as if it were not important. However, deep down I know that what I have to offer originates from my point of difference, from my French roots. To me, it is important. Being a Frenchman in New York is like living this constant paradox.

New York remains the global capital of the business world, and the advertising world especially. In all imaginable positions, we find people from all imaginable nationalities. Not only have I not been expected to slip into the American mold, I have been allowed to assume my origins. Sometimes this even means giving credence to some of the shortcomings commonly associated with my compatriots.

Latin impatience, for example, always creates a surprise this side of the Atlantic, not always a good one. In the same way, criticizing things, which comes so naturally to the French since their earliest school years, is badly perceived. And yet how can we move forward and progress without objectively analyzing past errors and recent problems? . . . However, people in America are quick to adopt ways of doing things that come from elsewhere when they see that they are effective. This is how they imported Disruption. It was born in France, a place that is not known for exporting best practices.

It comes to me as no surprise that Disruption, a method that seeks to create ruptures, emerged in my country. French philosophers have always legitimized contestation, held independent thinking in high regard, and demanded a constant questioning of conventions. School prepared us well.

French education also taught us to be interested in paradox. Paradox and Disruption are related. They share this tight tension, this telescoping of ideas that creates an unexpected spark, these pirouettes of thought that can capture our imagination.

As mentioned earlier, we recommended to Nextel a campaign that encouraged its clients to act more, to become "doers." As a result, the company encouraged its clients to talk, and thus to telephone, less. It is this paradox that creates the impact. Our agency in South Africa displayed billboards all over the country carrying the most disturbing photos of apartheid to denounce another contemporary form of apartheid, which is country folk who banish seropositive people from their villages. Here images that need to be buried once and for all have been exploited to serve a noble cause. It is the ultimate paradox.

At the end of the day, and even though it is rarely discussed, language remains a key topic, given the barriers it creates. No matter how hard we try to understand the true meaning behind the words of others, we will always be "foreign." Perfect bilingualism, a very rare thing, is required so that nothing is lost in translation. So we consistently feel frustrated and at a disadvantage when we are not expressing ourselves in our own mother tongue. We might as well admit it and get used to it, and remind ourselves that language is the secret zone within all of us, the point from which we construct our own world. It allows us first of all to explain our convictions and our passions to our very selves. Such as how I feel about working closely every day with people from different countries, different cultures, with people who, effectively, speak a thousand different languages.

*　　*　　*

"Atlantic culture" is an expression used to explain how New York watches Europe and Europe watches New York. This form of culture is at the core of most advertising networks. Born in New York, these networks have accompanied, sometimes even preceded, their American clients, often starting their expansion in Europe. This culture is also present within TBWA, except for one important nuance. Our biggest agency by far is based in Los Angeles. When they look across the sea, our people there are thinking of China and Japan, not Europe. This attraction is even stronger, given the fact that the agency counts Sony and Nissan among its most important clients.

Does a "Pacific culture" already exist? In any case, it is a force, an attraction. A "Pacific polarity" has taken on both a real and symbolic nature within our network. It reveals itself when we meet, when we exchange ideas, and when we work on campaigns together. Multiple cultural bridges are built from one continent to another, between Asia and America just as much as between Europe and Asia. I feel every day the two-way stretching of the network. Its center of gravity is unlike that of our competitors. It is more in line with the world as it is today. It allows, and even encourages, a higher level of diversity.

My desire is for TBWA to become one of the most multicultural companies in the world, the ultimate melting pot. This is one condition that our agency has to meet to become one of the most interesting things happening in the industry.

As Philippe Michel, one of my most brilliant French colleagues, would have said, "The talent that counts is the talent of the other."

PART II

Acting Differently

5

Culture

(Or How a Company Culture Can Become Its Key Competitive Asset)

"Culture is just not one aspect of the game, it *is* the game," said Lou Gerstner, the former chief executive officer of IBM and the inspiration for one of the most memorable corporate turnarounds of all time. In making this statement, he found a striking way to insist on how important culture is to corporate life.

Any culture, corporate or not, is the fruit of a collective adventure. Something created through the combined sensitivities and intelligence of thousands of men and women. Something shared. A mental structure, an evolving language, a collection of desires, a kind of *élan*. A view of the future based on values of the past. If you feel comfortable with this definition, you will agree that every enterprise ends up creating its own culture.

Everyone recognizes Apple's culture, which is both anti-establishment and elitist . . . a kind of contradiction in terms, but an attractive contradiction. A few months ago, Richard Branson climbed down the facade of the Virgin Megastore on the Champs Elysees, to remind us of his company's character, which he describes as "audacious and uncomplexed" . . . In a sector that is extremely fast-moving, Google also demonstrates the force of a corporate culture. Its search engine may have become the world's biggest advertising machine, yet the company never forgets that it was founded by engineers, champions of the algorithm. And this desire for scientific excellence never wanes . . . The specific cultures of many companies such as Ikea, Southwest Airlines, General Electric, Starbucks, and The Body Shop are also well known; each culture is unique, and it has been examined closely for years by leading business analysts.

I would like to mention here some company cultures which are not often cited, being less familiar this side of the Atlantic, but which for me are exemplary. Two I know very well, since they have been clients for over twenty years, Danone and Michelin, and another one of them where I myself enjoy being the client, that is to say Hermès.

First, Michelin. The laws of physics are such that it is impossible for a tire producer to obtain the highest performance during the first miles of a tire's life and to maximize this performance over time. Automobile manufacturers, the tire makers' principal customers, insist on obtaining the optimal performance at the beginning of a tire's life. The aim is to maximize the car's road-holding performance and give automotive journalists the greatest impression of safety when they test new car models. Michelin has always refused to play this game. It has always given priority to maintaining performance over time, even if this means being initially slightly less competitive for the very few first miles of the tire's life. In other words, Michelin refuses to sacrifice driver safety, not even by the most infinitesimal amount, over the long term. Respect for the customer is at the very heart of the company. It is the central point of Michelin's culture. If you want to define this culture even more precisely, you could say it is both rigid and respectful.

Selling yogurts, fermented dairy products that facilitated the digestion, Danone was initially available only through pharmacies. This fact determined the company's future direction; since then, it has never wavered from its commitment to health. Even though the company has launched more pleasure-based products, creams or desserts, it continued to invest in its quest for healthy eating. In creating the Danone Health Institute, as we have already discussed, it took on the mission of better understanding the relationship between eating and health; it sponsored doctors, scientists, and researchers. And every year the knowledge on these issues has been enriched. Over time, Danone's management increased the number of initiatives in this vein, such as giving support to Nobel Prize winner Muhammad Yunus, inventor of microcredits. Danone has built dozens of microfactories in underdeveloped countries, where yogurts are produced at a price that makes them affordable to people with extremely low incomes. Through programs such as these, and through many others, Danone proves it is concerned and committed, two character traits that come from the company's health heritage. Concerned and committed . . .

I was reading a piece the other day in which Jean-Louis Dumas, the emblematic boss of Hermès (or should I say "the House of Hermès"?) said, among other things: "We produce items that are costly rather than expensive." Or even: "We are neither in the luxury world, nor in fashion." His successor talks about "a project for poetry in an economic universe." For Hermès, beauty is at the core of the company. It is this beauty that has created the permanence of the brand. One of its slogans claimed: *Nothing changes, everything changes*. In fact, Hermès has a particular relationship with time. The brand does not seek to be of this time; it gives time to time. Fashion changes, Hermès remains, as if impervious to passing distractions. When all is said and done, Hermès is the epitome of the culture of perennity.

I speak in more detail of these three companies because I want to underline an important point: A corporate culture cannot be created out of nothing. From the outset, Michelin imposed upon itself very strict policies concerning safety. From the beginning, Danone decided to sell products that were proven to contribute to a balanced diet. From the very early days, Hermès set as an objective to be the reference in terms of quality. Every time an uncompromising product philosophy is adopted, an embryo of culture is created. Like a founding act, or rather, a founding behavior. From there the culture is enriched, nourished by the everyday events in the life of the enterprise. In this way, it conjugates values and know-how.

What is true for Michelin, Danone or Hermès, we strive for also at TBWA. Culture has been a key factor in the life of our agency. We too seek to combine skills with a way of behaving. A certain expertise, and a set of values . . . Drawing a parallel between major companies and

114

our agency could be seen as presumptuous, the comparison could be judged hazardous—but at our level as well, it is culture that makes the difference.

The explanation can be partly found in John Kotter and James Heskett's "Corporate Culture and Performance." In it, they demonstrate that the influence of corporate culture increases in direct proportion to the degree of competition in the market. And there are few markets as competitive as advertising. The fiercely fought battles to win new clients is a daily reminder. There is no critical mass needed to compete. A newcomer can, in the space of a few weeks, challenge the best-established agencies. Few markets are as open. In this business environment, a strong culture can reveal itself more powerful than one imagines. In certain cases, it can even become the ultimate competitive edge.

A COMMON PHILOSOPHY

A culture only becomes legitimized over time. But as we have seen, the very first years are crucial. They set the tone, light the way forward. It happens that our three agencies, TBWA, Chiat/Day, and BDDP had, from the outset, a very close vision of the business.

Firstly, all three had decided to belong to that most exclusive of clubs, the world's most creative agencies. I know of no agencies that started off less creative than they became. You cannot climb up the value chain in this way. I do know, unfortunately, of a number of creative agencies that have given up, since staying creative is a constant struggle. Anything but a God-given gift. Chiat/Day, TBWA, and

BDDP were creative from the very first day. And they remained so, ten, twenty years after, never losing their souls despite the turmoil of financial summersaults and successive mergers they lived through.

Above all, the three agencies possessed an embryonic common philosophy. For them, creative talent, whereas absolutely essential, alone is not enough. The strategies, the briefs given to the creative teams, also needed to be creative in themselves. The three agencies shared the desire to imagine unique strategies that sought to be intelligent (and the word "intelligent" does not overstate the case). TBWA surprised people with its campaigns for Evian in France, Lego in England, and Absolut in the United States. Chiat/Day invigorated the American advertising industry with its campaigns for Apple, ABC, Nike, Energizer. . . . And BBDP distinguished itself by bringing new perspectives to Danone, McDonald's, and the French Railways. None of these agencies were satisfied by creating advertising that would be seen as merely "creative." Each was also determined to be creative at the strategic level, which is the foundation of the concept of Disruption.

In fact, although each of our three agencies had a distinct and strong personality, they also shared the same sort of culture. They had so much in common that they were made to be together. It was almost as if they were promised to each other. Predestined.

Indeed, we had considered joining our forces as early as 1986, when my partners and I, at the time the managers of BDDP, first contacted TBWA. We had a deep respect for what Bill Tragos, the spirited leader of the agency, had accomplished along with his three partners. During the previous decade, TBWA had achieved a brilliant expansion across most of Europe. The negotiations almost succeeded. But only almost.

In the years that followed, Omnicom bought successively TBWA, Chiat/Day, and finally BDDP. What is interesting in all this was that before being acquired, BDDP had only ever approached two companies in view of a possible merger. The first was TBWA, and the second, as you will have understood, was Chiat/Day.

Sharing the same idea, to join the best in the market to rapidly build a worldwide network, we met Jay Chiat and Lee Clow in 1987. We wanted to buy their agency, and they wanted to get their hands on ours. We failed to persuade ourselves one way or the other. And nothing came out of it. We did not reach an agreement, but remained good friends.

We had multiplied the contacts among our three companies in the past. We knew each other well and saw each other as business friends. In short, we somehow believed that it would be intelligent for us to find a way to do something together. We knew full well that mergers are rarely successful. In our industry, they were practically sure to fail. The advertising industry is like a graveyard of dozens of great agencies whose cultures and energy have disappeared in badly conceived mergers. But the three of us felt differently about one another, because we knew we shared very close cultures.

Eventually, what we had not managed to make happen by ourselves was imposed on us by the market. It was our shared inability to succeed in becoming truly international on our own that eventually brought us together. It was as if our union had been preordained.

TBWA, THE MULTICULTURAL
MELTING POT

TBWA was different from the outset. It was neither born at the turn of the century nor founded in a major advertising capital, such as New York or London. TBWA was collectively conceived by an Italian, an American, a Frenchman, and a Swiss, all of whom were determined to avoid a national bias or to become entrenched in any one country— very telling of the TBWA story we are living today.

An unlikely group, hailing from very different backgrounds, they knew they were on to something great. From the outset they decided that they would break the mold as the first equally partnered multinational and multidisciplined agency. They launched TBWA on August 11, 1970.

As luck would have it, the media fell in love with TBWA because of its originality. In early autumn of 1970, the founders were given the equivalent of several million dollars worth of free media to launch the agency. With posters plastered all over Paris, they had radio coverage, they had magazine articles, they had an incredible PR presence.

To appreciate the scope of what they embarked on, it is important to realize that, during the 1970s in Europe, advertising agencies were national. The few international groups were generally American. So this European fledgling paved the way as the first multicultural and multinational network.

After the initial opening in Paris, it was a short eight months before the second agency was established in Milan, Italy. TBWA management wanted to move fast, to avoid being associated with any one country. The opening of the German and British offices soon followed.

The four founders showed a great talent for convincing the greatest creative minds of the time to join them. I have already spoken of the founders of BBH in London. I also should mention Michael Conrad in Germany, later to become chief creative officer of Leo Burnett Worldwide and Hunt/Lascaris, the best agency in South Africa—the agency that Nelson Mandela chose for his election campaign—led by one of the most famous creative directors in the world, John Hunt. And let us not forget Ernesto Savaglio in Argentina, José Alberto Téran in Mexico, and Trevor Beattie, one of the most famous admen in the United Kingdom after Charles Saatchi, and the man behind Tony Blair's last election campaigns. Scott Whybin's agency in Melbourne joined in 1996. This was our first agency in that part of the world and was the spearhead of our network in Asia. Under the leadership of Keith Smith, Asia became the fastest-growing region in our network, with TBWA being the fastest-growing network there.

CHIAT/DAY, CALIFORNIA DREAMING

Guy Day and Jay Chiat were running two small agencies in Los Angeles at a time when everyone knew that the advertising centers were New York and Chicago. One day Guy Day phoned Jay Chiat. They had never met, but Day said that he liked Chiat's work and suggested a meeting. Chiat agreed and invited him over.

Some weeks later, on April 1, 1968, they merged their operation into Chiat/Day. Within a month, they were asked to pitch for their first major piece of consumer business, the Equitable Savings Bank, a big opportunity and their first success.

In many ways, the growth of the agency has reflected the strength of Southern California as a creative community. Then came the real estate boom, the growth and expansion of Japanese business, and the ubiquity of Silicon Valley, bringing with it the emergence of computers and high technology.

The agency lived by the motto "Creative is not a Department," which was always upheld, not just by management but by everyone. In the media department for instance, the well-known opinion was "If it doesn't exist, we'll invent it." Apple's advertising changed the way business talked to business, introduced the world to the personal computer, and reinvented the role of the SuperBowl along the way. And before Nike and the Energizer Bunny, if you asked people what category would be doing the most creative advertising on television in the future, they probably would not have chosen athletic shoes or batteries. . . . The end result is that Chiat/Day has made it permissible for companies to seek out creativity and great advertising in any category of product, and in cities other than New York and Chicago.

Forty years after its creation, Chiat/Day, now TBWA\Chiat\Day, is remarkable in many ways. It is the number-one ranking agency in California. It is also one of the three or four most creative agencies in the history of advertising in the United States. And it is one of the very rare agencies that manages to be both brilliantly creative and deeply international. It has a huge influence on the network because a great number of our international clients are handled from its Plaza del Rey office: Apple, Adidas, Nissan, PlayStation, and Mars to name but a few.

But above all, the Los Angeles office is led by Lee Clow, who was at Chiat/Day from the early years and has become the "symbolic cofounder." Without him, the campaigns described in this book would have never seen the light of day—nor would this book itself.

Having always been curious about what was happening across the Atlantic, I have studied Chiat/Day's advertising since 1984. As I analyzed their campaigns in great detail, I always remembered the text by Ralph Waldo Emerson used in the voice-over for Reebok's advertising: "There is a time in every man's education when he arrives at the conviction that envy is ignorance, that imitation is suicide, that he must take himself for better or worse . . . Insist on yourself. Never imitate."

At the time, Chiat/Day had a reputation for being very creative but too outrageous and not sound enough strategically. It was quite unfair and far from the truth because very early on the agency had invested in a strong strategic planning department. In fact, Jane Newman had made history in American advertising by creating and managing the first strategic planning department in the United States, based on the English model. Very few American agencies had such a sharp perception of brands and how to build them to last, using wit and tact.

The legacy of Chiat/Day is the passion to go further, to refuse all forms of conformity. No one represented this better than Jay Chiat himself. He always saw things differently, and never hesitated to destabilize his friends, partners, or clients.

At the center was the belief that "good enough is not enough." Building a great company required dedication that had to be embraced by everyone, everyday—regardless of job title, the challenge, or even the discomfort. It was this dedication and long hours that led to jokes about the agency's true name being "Chiat/Day & Night."

THE RISE AND FALL OF BDDP

On January 2, 1984, when my three partners and I launched BDDP, we announced our plan to build an international network and to become a leader in the French industry, along with Havas and Publicis. This launch was an unprecedented success. In just five years, agency revenues had reached $80 million, reportedly the highest organic growth rate ever seen for a new agency in Europe, and apparently anywhere else. I can recount these facts without the risk of being called arrogant, since a few years later, financial problems wiped out the sum of our commercial achievements. It was an unforgivable reversal.

From the outset, we wanted to create a strong company, not just a good advertising agency. This aim was manifested in different ways: by a positioning that was unique at the time, based on strategic creativity; by investing a high percentage of our revenue into training; and by having one Apple desktop computer per every two employees, an unheard-of ratio at the time. We were not pioneers in advertising, we were pioneers in managing an advertising agency.

By the middle of our short lifetime, our stated goal of being in the top ten worldwide networks was not out of our reach. For a non-quoted company without access to public funding, this would have been an exceptional performance. Our story, alas, ended very differently. To understand it, we need to examine the context.

We were based in the French market, which is ten times smaller than the American market and represents only 4 percent of the worldwide market. Starting from scratch, we could count on neither the support of major international clients nor the leverage of the stock exchange. (The French financial community had a much more reserved view of advertising agencies than did its British counterparts.) And so, with the odds more than stacked against us, we started out by setting ourselves an almost unattainable objective: We would not buy a worldwide network but build one, brick by brick, country by country. And fast. Fast, that is, compared to the likes of Ogilvy and J. Walter Thompson, who took forty or fifty years to build their networks.

1994 was a pivotal year. It was the year when a great adventure turned into a much less glorious story. After having taken control of more than twenty agencies around the world, including the third largest in New York, we had accumulated a debt of almost $200 million, a burden too heavy for our company to bear. We found ourselves short of capital and strapped by lack of cash flow.

We had run out of steam and were unable to avoid the inevitable. The bankers announced the end of our saga. Investors manifested themselves, renegotiated our debt, and took control of our company. Hardly a year after having bought us, they put us back on the block. This was a dreadful blow, coming much too close to the previous one. We quickly conceived a plan where GGT would acquire us, and we presented it as a *fait accompli* to our short-term shareholders. Over time, however, GGT too overreached itself and also put us up for sale.

In 1998 we were absorbed by Omnicom, the worldwide advertising giant that today employs over sixty thousand people and that had earlier already pursued BDDP. If we had to lose the control of our company, it could not have happened in a better way. Omnicom is known as being the best communications group in the world by far. All advertising professionals and financial analysts would agree on this point.

The sale was concluded March 1. John Wren, the chief executive of Omnicom, universally acknowledged as the leading force in our industry, decided to merge us with the smallest of its networks, TBWA.

The financial community had condemned us in February 1994. It was the beginning of a very painful period for me. It ended in April 2001, when I found myself at the head of TBWA.

COMPANY CULTURE

The years went by, and little by little, TBWA, the fruit of all these mergers, became stronger. Today we are a company of ten thousand people and enjoy a very strong growth rate. TBWA's vitality is due to a number of factors, not the least of which is its entrepreneurial past and the legendary creative talent of Lee Clow. But there is another factor, less obvious, somewhat subjective. I am talking of our culture. Over time, we have created a way of doing things, a culture that has become our own.

The three agencies, TBWA, Chiat/Day and BDDP, at one moment or another in their histories, had all endured very destabilizing times. Yet despite the uncertainties, the trials and tribulations, they had managed to maintain some sort of vitality, of tension, and refused to let go of what was essential. In other words, the cultures of our companies survived and have even been reinforced. We could have expected quite the opposite; usually when a company is acquired, its culture becomes diluted and more often than not is reduced to next to nothing.

As I have already stated, over time, it became clear that the cultures of the three agencies were very similar. This is what made it possible for them to blend into one, forming a unique set of values that our company stands for, values that are shared by our employees the world over.

I have already mentioned Lou Gerstner and his way of seeing the importance of culture in business. Jim Stengel, from Procter & Gamble, spoke in a similar vein in addressing university students: "In the end, building a business . . . is about building a culture."

Our business is about imagination. Nevertheless, I believe that culture is more influential than imagination. It is our *way* of doing things rather than what we do, that makes the difference. In our profession, there are no factories and no patents. The difference is made by those who make up the company and the culture that unites them. Though company culture is important in every industry, it is crucial in intangible industries such as ours.

A strong company culture is not just a soft option to add value, or a topic of discussion for the authors of management books, or an attempt to bring intelligence, warmth, and sensitivity to the cold world of business. Quite the opposite. A company culture is a key competitive factor. No sustainable growth can be maintained in a cultural wasteland, no real future achieved without a view on the role of the company and its place in society. We need an answer to the question: What would our industry lose if my company no longer existed? We need to answer this question without arrogance, but without false modesty either. If you cannot answer this question, one day or another you will be faced with a problem of growth. You will always be two or three points behind, and it will be too late. A culture cannot be improvised: As we have seen earlier, it only becomes legitimate against the test of time.

Over the years, our culture has become more precise, refined, enriched. One of the ambitions of this book is to show that a company culture is multidimensional, because it is about bringing together values and skills. Inherent to us is a particular attitude, an ability and desire to challenge general convention, which is what we call a "disruptive attitude." Our culture stems from these two words. They are a constant, a key, the lens through which we can examine everything we do and plan to do.

David Maister, former Harvard Business School professor and member of the Omnicom University Faculty, has conducted several studies analyzing the relationship between employee satisfaction and company profits. He has studied hundreds of service companies and interviewed thousands of people. His conclusion is unequivocal: "Offices with strong corporate cultures enjoy the highest employee satisfaction, and offices with the highest employee satisfaction are the most profitable ones."

Our network is made up of 238 offices. The number is big enough to confirm that statistically, at TBWA, this correlation is a reality.

A BEAUTIFUL NETWORK

As I mentioned, I was handed the reins of TBWA in 2001. At the time, Andy McMains, a highly respected journalist at *Adweek*, asked me: "How does it feel being at the head of a loose federation of local agencies?" I did not like the question, which is not to say there was not an element of truth in it. TBWA was not really a network, but rather a juxtaposition, a mosaic of brilliant agencies. Over the following years, our organization was revamped from top to bottom, our business model was transformed, and we changed the way we managed our global clients.

The fact remains that our network includes an impressive number of talented local agencies, probably more than any other network, agencies that are well known to advertising professionals around the world. We have all heard of the long-established American networks but know little if anything about their individual agencies. Those of TBWA in Los Angeles, London, Johannesburg, Paris, and Bangkok to name a few are in the trade press on a weekly basis.

I have written about more than twenty of our network agencies. TBWA\Chiat\Day in Los Angeles is the most innovative; TBWA\New York, the most provocative; TBWA\Thailand, the most creative; TBWA\Korea, the most emotional; TBWA\Shanghai, the most surprising; TBWA\Finland, the most entrepreneurial; TBWA\Mexico, the most seductive; TBWA\Paris, the most awarded; and TBWA\Hunt\Lascaris in Johannesburg, the most inspiring . . .

I remember having said one day: "Let's not believe too much in our own public relations." Doing so can only lead to complacency. But this aside, I cannot help but be proud of the awards that we have won around the world. I will engage in what is effectively self-congratulation here, without false modesty. I would like to think that the hardships we have endured over the last ten years, those painful years that have led us to where we are today, give me permission to do so.

In a memo I sent out to the network at the beginning of 2005, I highlighted the impressive number of awards we had amassed. We were voted Global Network of the Year by *Advertising Age*. Our Los Angeles office was named American Agency of the Year by *Adweek*. TBWA\Asia-Pacific was elected Regional Network of the Year. The Global Network was the most awarded at the Cannes Advertising Festival by far, taking home the Grand Prix, agency of the year, as well as the greatest number of Lions. Twenty-three of our individual agencies around the world were named agency of the year. I concluded my memo with the eternal adage that it is harder to stay on top than to get there. In the words of Truman Capote: "It is better to aim for the sky than to be up there."

If 2004 was a particularly gratifying year in terms of awards, 2005 was the year we truly arrived: No. 1 at Cannes, No. 1 at the Effies (effectiveness awards), No. 1 in the *Gunn Report* (the ranking of all rankings).

From the outside, this recitation may appear a little hollow. A profession that chooses to celebrate itself could look a bit narcissistic. Perhaps. But awards are important. If they were not, why have Procter & Gamble and McDonald's decided to attend Cannes for several years now, with a large number of other marketers quickly following suit? Our clients are on the hunt for the most creative agencies. At this time of extraordinarily competitive markets, companies understand once and for all the added value that creativity brings. And they are well aware that agencies that rarely win awards are unlikely to be ahead of their time.

Awards create a virtuous circle. Good agencies attract the best creative minds, who win awards, which attract other great creative thinkers, who in turn make the agency even better.

* * *

We need to carry on like this, helping our creative people to express the best of their talent, in the best interests of our clients. It looks like we are on the right track; as I write this, the past twelve months have proven to be remarkable. After receiving the Agency of the Year award in Cannes, we were named Global Network of the Year by *AdWeek* and ranked No. 1 in *Advertising Age*'s A List.

TBWA today is much larger than it was ten years ago, just after its merger with Chiat/Day and before its merger with BDDP. I can still remember the question that Jay Chiat was asking himself back then: "I'd like to know how big we can be before we get bad."

I hope I will never know the answer.

6

Values

(Or How Company Values that Come at No Cost Have No Worth)

In client meetings back in the 1980s, you could be almost certain that the subject of Corporate Mission Statements would be brought up for discussion. I can still remember today's head of Auchan, number two in the French retail industry behind Carrefour, telling us he had picked our agency because we seemed to be capable of putting together such a statement for him.

It was the fashionable concept at the time. These statements were a way of reconciling, on the one hand, business objectives, such as increasing market share, and, on the other, less tangible objectives: A company has to have values. But in the end everyone was laying claim to the same ones, as there simply were not that many to choose from. The concept and what people did with it became gradually commoditized.

Yet no one believes more in company values than I. If this notion has been rendered somewhat banal, that does not make it any less important. Values will always play a major role in business life—provided that they are taken seriously and not treated as a kind of spiritual veneer for a company lacking communications substance. On the contrary, I believe they must be put at the heart of the company, becoming part of its DNA, its genetic capital.

The very ambiguity of the word "value" is meaningful. It signifies both financial value and human values. Value is created through values, nothing comes for free. As the founder of DDB, Bill Bernbach, once said: "A principle isn't a principle until it costs you money."

This belief certainly applies to transparency, a quality that lies at the very heart of our company.

TRANSPARENCY

Twenty years ago, in many countries, the advertising industry had fallen into bad habits. Advertising executives had identified multiple sources of additional income over and above the official commissions paid by clients. It was more often than not unofficial income, sorts of kickbacks offered by all types of suppliers.

This dubious way of working was by no means uncommon. All my French colleagues were indulging in it. But it took me a long time to realize that these questionable activities were not just found in Latin countries. Imagination knows no boundaries when large sums of money are involved. In fact, this was happening all over the world, with the possible exception of the United States, but I am not even sure about that.

Today this graft has mostly disappeared. But back then, it was common practice.

When we started up our own agency, from the very first day, we took a stand against this way of doing business and guaranteed our clients total transparency.

We asked Arthur Andersen to audit our accounts and to testify to our clients that this transparency was real. This was back in 1984, and at that time we were pioneers. The concept of transparency was an unknown value, and the trend of ethical companies was not yet widespread.

Very quickly our position became known by the press, triggering the wrath of our main competitors. We had hit them where it hurts. Press articles were numerous. For more than two years the subject appeared frequently on the front pages of the economic press. In one interview I went as far as to talk about "godfathers" and "mafia" to describe some of my opponents. The battle was harsh, and we emerged from it with some deep scars.

But we were sure that we were right and that we were acting in the best interests of the industry. One of the consequences of these years of turmoil, where we had to face incredible pressure—sometimes even personal threats—was to strengthen my conviction on the importance of company values and the key role they play in the positive development of an enterprise.

Transparency was our foundation. We had decided from the very beginning that strong ethics would be an integral part of our company. But make no mistake, we were not merely motivated by morality. "Ethics are the inner aesthetics," Pierre Reverdy, a French poet associated with surrealism and cubism, once said. This idea guided us. We wanted, and I still want, to build a company that is beautiful.

Our financial transparency led us to adopt transparent behavior in many other areas. And at the end of the day, this principle is what matters most. It has influenced everything we have touched, our attitudes, our behavior, our relationships with people as much as, if not more than, our relationship with money. I guess we can call it integrity. For us, integrity means being transparent in the way we talk to our clients and our people. It means being brave enough to tell our clients what we really think—usually with diplomacy but always with determination. It means telling our people what we expect from them—giving them a clear picture of what we want them to accomplish, being straight with them, avoiding manipulation.

Years, decades have gone by. But transparency is still one of the values that are key to us. The two other values are audacity and open-mindedness. I have to admit that these may not appear to be blindingly original. But as I pointed out earlier, there are not that many values to choose from. What really counts is action. It is easy to pontificate on one value or another, but actions need to follow words. We need to render values valuable, even costly, both psychologically and financially. I certainly remember the price we paid for standing up against our own industry practices.

The same goes for audacity. In a service industry, we need to be "ready to serve," an attitude that can quickly lead to subservience. You need a certain amount of courage to consistently tell your client or employee what you really think.

As for open-mindedness, it is a source of our true enrichment. It means caring more for what we have yet to learn than for what we already know. The main thing is to keep on learning from others.

AUDACITY

During a press conference in the early days of BDDP, we made it very clear that we wanted to become one of the top three agencies in France and to create an international network. People considered us determined rather than presumptuous. Laying down such an objective made it credible and thus possible, even likely to happen. Going by today's credo, where image precedes reality, we were seen as the future big players of the industry. The writing was on the wall even before our campaigns were.

In a staff speech I gave recently, I made it clear that I saw nothing to prevent TBWA from climbing to the very top of the global agency rankings. If we stayed true to our values and principles, it would only be a matter of time. But this clear focus is the very condition that is always the hardest to meet. It is so easy to get distracted.

Developing creative work is the time when we especially need to be audacious. Some are quick to give up. The most mediocre of agencies sometimes employ talented creative people who would have succeeded in agencies elsewhere. Complacency, alas, all too often prevails: Agencies give clients what they expect, no more, no less. Yet any campaign worthy of its name needs to make a *creative leap*, as I have said in the past, or put another way, a leap into the unknown. If you do not feel at least a little bit anxious when presented with a creative idea, then it has little chance of creating impact and making its mark, and it will join the pile of unengaging messages cluttering up our screens.

Lee Clow often speaks of "brave thinking," and here is what he says:

Each one of us must be brave in everything we accomplish for our clients and for our company. Brave thinking rejects the resignation, the "good enough" mentality that characterizes conventional thinking. It exalts the unexpected and welcomes change. Ambition is what drives us to devise new solutions, to seek out better ways of doing, to set higher standards. Ambition raises our sights and opens us up to change and new ideas. It drives us to better serve our clients and our own business. In our personal lives, it is the desire to live to the fullest and make the most of ourselves.

In our values, ambition is in balance with integrity. It is vital to keep a proper tension between these two. Ambition without integrity is political. Ambition without integrity does not consider the needs of others. Ambition without integrity survives only in the short term. Ambition alone is selfish, but ambition linked with integrity benefits everyone.

OPEN-MINDEDNESS

The third value that we strive to defend daily is open-mindedness. Openness toward others, toward their differences, the way they are and the way they act, is something that needs to be firmly rooted within us all. It seems difficult to imagine not adhering to such a universal value. And yet how many companies show themselves as closed, self-absorbed, inward-looking? Such companies build up walls between themselves and the outside world.

Open-mindedness implies curiosity and respect. Tom Peters, author of *In Search of Excellence* and more recently *Re-imagine*, talks about *curiosity workers* in defining the role of company employees in the twenty-first century. People working in these companies cannot progress unless they show an interest in what other offices and countries can bring them. Allowing ourselves to be truly curious, and opening up our minds without prejudice, creates real pleasure, a kind of jubilation.

Our agency is fortunate enough to have a presence in nearly one hundred countries. For those willing to make the effort, there is always something to learn across the border. Belonging to an international network gives us a continuous flow of opportunities to enrich ourselves.

That being said, I am often amazed by the lack of curiosity demonstrated by some people on both sides of the Atlantic. This is why I have taken numerous initiatives to change this, to make each side open up toward each other.

The American market has vast resources. Companies here are able to specialize more than anywhere else. It is the opposite for agencies in smaller countries such as France. Let us take the example of the event marketing agencies, this is instructive: When McDonald's organizes its biennial franchisee conventions, fifteen thousand people are brought together in the same room. Only the cities of Orlando and Las Vegas have facilities big enough to accommodate them. Services for this event are divided up between multiple providers: an event planning agency for logistics (hotels, buses, convention room reservations); an exhibition company to set up the exhibitions for McDonald's suppliers—who number over a hundred; a production agency for the setup and technical production of the show; a corporate agency to write speeches; a talent agency to advise on suitable speakers; several other local agencies to organize evening events such as gala dinners and the like. In Paris, London, or Shanghai, one single agency would take care of everything. The agency would work professionally, certainly, but probably not with the same degree of expertise as the Americans with their extreme levels of specialization.

In 1996, when I published the book *Disruption* in the United States, I was looking for a press agent who specialized in management books. I was told that this search was too wide. I said more specifically marketing books. Still too broad, I was told. Finally I was advised to look for someone specializing in advertising publications. Several persons in New York specialized in handling press relations just for advertising books. You never see this level of specialization outside of the United States.

This is why I believe that, nine times out of ten, the state of art of any communications discipline will be found this side of the Atlantic. Specialization very often leads to a higher level of expertise. Europeans would benefit from being quicker to learn about the latest developments in America. They need to be a little more curious.

In contrast, the limited resources in a large part of the world have led to new forms of entrepreneurship. Countries outside the United States, with less means, ask themselves different kinds of questions. For example, integration, the capacity to optimize resources between the diverse disciplines in communications, has been a serious issue in the United States only for the last ten years, whereas our agency in South Africa was developing systems of optimization between disciplines over twenty years ago. In France, we set up our direct marketing arm, Tequila, in 1985, barely one year after the birth of BDDP. We were "integrated from the outset."

The limited size of the national advertising markets, such as those in South Africa or France, stimulates this desire to take new initiatives. Agencies in these countries are forced to invent different forms of activity to achieve growth . . . And they find it surprising to see so many articles on "integration" being published in the American trade press today, as if it were a new idea. Articles on the same subject could have been found in the international press a long time ago.

In 1991 I had a discussion in Cincinnati with John Smale, the chief executive officer of Procter & Gamble who had just retired. I asked him a question regarding the evolution of marketing techniques: "What is different today compared to when you started out." He responded with an anecdote.

As a young brand manager handling Crest toothpaste, he had suggested the launch of a Crest toothbrush. The idea was complete heresy at the time. "A brand for every product and a product for every brand," as the decades-old P&G credo went. His suggestion was therefore refused. A few days before our meeting, some forty years later, Crest had just launched its own toothbrush. Over time, it had gradually become too expensive to launch a new brand for each new product. And so it was more effective to create an umbrella brand covering a range of products. By doing this, a brand would have more weight and meaning. Economic reality had hit Crest.

This same reality had hit Europe some twenty years earlier. Per capita advertising spending was much lower. Certain products just could not generate the media spending required to create a new brand. As a result, we created a number of umbrella brands. I can remember making several recommendations to our clients, starting with Danone, on this subject: How to extend the brand without diluting it? How to introduce new products without losing the brand essence? We were creating a new expertise twenty years ahead of some other countries. I still recall the management supervisor of Oil of Olay in New York, a brand that has gone from one core product in the 1980s to a range of eighty-five products on the market today, coming to Paris to study several recommendations we had put together on problems similar to those facing him at the time.

A last example: media buying. The English media still credit the Saatchi brothers with the invention of media companies, based on their launch of Zenith Media in the 1980s. But in fact we all know that this discipline was born in France at the end of the 1960s and that it only finally took off in the United States in the mid-1990s. Just as I suggested to Europeans, Americans would do well to take more of an interest, and more quickly, in what is happening across the Atlantic.

The parallel between the rest of the world and America is instructive. Europeans are often a step ahead, whereas Americans push their level of expertise further. Yet instead of learning from each other with an open mind, we often do the exact opposite. We pretend to act interested, then go on with business as usual the minute we have turned our backs.

The other side of curiosity is respect. The oldest American networks, those born before the Second World War, exported their corporate culture and their Americanism in their way of being and doing. Other American networks, often the more recent ones, may act as if they are multicultural, but their leaders still show a superficial or contrived attitude towards "international." They leap on the initiatives taken by their Swedish or Thai agencies, but forget all about them once comfortably back in New York.

Complacency is a barrier to open-mindedness. Our aim is to build a different kind of network, one that is different because it is born out of the idea of observing different cultures and learning from them, without trying to homogenize everything. The diversity of our cultures brings a unique richness to our company. We began to understand a long time ago that "the future can come from anywhere."

* * *

Whatever the company you work for, your dream, one way or another, should be of building something different, something with its own identity, something compelling. As Henry Ford said: "A business that is in the business of making only money is a poor kind of business." I believe that a company such as ours is defined more by its values—integrity, audacity, and open-mindedness—than by its mere functions, which cover all the communications disciplines and are practiced by all our competitors.

In March 2003 we brought together four hundred network managers for a two-day session in Los Angeles. There we witnessed a series of presentations and speeches by various managers of our agency. We also had the honor of welcoming two special guests, Frank Gehry and Steve Jobs.

Frank Gehry had come to talk to us about creativity and to explain how ideas come to life in one of the most modern and forward-thinking architectural firms in the world. He was tired after spending the night on a plane, but he lit up when presenting the projects that resulted in the Bilbao museum. We were in awe, most of us incapable of deciphering his series of sketches that only the young architects under his wing could have a chance of understanding. He explained to us the vision he had for creating volumes. He saw them as sculptures, enormous and limitless. We were admiring creativity, in its purest form.

The following day Steve Jobs spoke to us for over an hour, an hour in which he talked spontaneously about courage and values. He was as brilliant as usual, perhaps more than usual, addressing a spellbound audience behind closed doors. There is one piece of advice he gave that day that I remember particularly well: "Have the courage to be who you are . . . I think most companies have completely forgotten that . . . 'Management by Value.' You want to hire people with the same values as you and even though you might argue a lot, you know you're trying to go to the same place."

I often browse the shelves of bookshops devoted to management books. I have read and reread the greatest authors: Peter Drucker, Tom Peters, Michael Porter, and in particular Gary Hamel. Nowadays there are certain words and phrases they no longer use, words that have been beaten to death, such as paradigm, vision, competitive advantage, key competencies, mission statements . . . and also value. Yet for me this last word remains essential, irreplaceable, despite how outmoded it may sound. It describes what should be at the heart of a company, outlining its attitude, if not its soul: these values that create value.

Mark Kelleher, chairman of Southwest Airlines, the most successful airline in the United States, advises: "hire attitude, teach skills." He is right. We focus too much on the skills and talents we want to recruit, without concerning ourselves enough with what people might think about or expect from their life within our company, without checking if they will fit in with the culture in which they are about to be immersed.

And we never fail to regret it.

7

Skills

(Or How Our Company Has Nurtured Special Skills)

Staff speeches punctuate our corporate life. Not only can they serve to get things back on track, but they can also be instrumental in giving the system a "kick-start," guiding the company along the right path and defining its common goal.

I have delivered several such speeches since our different companies came together in 1998, each of which was intended to chart our progress along our chosen route. These can be speeches where I share our vision of the industry or the agency, or sorts of rallying cries such as a sales manager might give to motivate the troops.

The speech I gave in Madrid in 2001 was entitled: "What Does Success Look Like?" In it I gave a detailed explanation of what I saw as the virtues of our business model and organizational structure. I stressed the effectiveness of our creative product and recalled our reason for being: "Our mission is to make our clients famous for the ideas they stand for. The famous idea that can drive a company forward for many years." I concluded by suggesting the diverse criteria that would allow us to measure our performance, our success, over the following five years.

In Los Angeles, in March 2003, I gave the opening speech of a conference that took place only a few days before the beginning of hostilities in Iraq. I remember saying that we had together in the room all different shades of opinion. We ourselves represented all parts of the world. But we all knew that the first step toward a peaceful world comes with the understanding of other cultures, with the understanding of each other. "This is what we call tolerance," I added. I went on to welcome everyone to the only city in the world housing a Tolerance Museum. It was Stanislas de Quercize, former president of Cartier New York, who had given me its West Pico Boulevard address.

The theme of my speech that day was "right place, right time." The industry had just emerged from two very painful years. We worked through those years with our eyes on the future, and we never stopped investing. I remember the memorable quote from Sam Walton, founder of Wal-Mart: "The recession? I've decided not to join in."

I reflected on what we had achieved, believing that we would emerge stronger from these difficult years, and I concluded by saying:

The result is that we are increasingly a network like no other, with a unified personality and a different culture. My objective is that when your family or your friends ask you about TBWA, you can reply: "I work for a very special company." And in a few years, when you look back and reflect on your days at TBWA, you will think: "I was at the right place, at the right time."

It is good to allow people to become carried along and uplifted by the enthusiasm of this sort of meeting. Such exuberance is justified if it is sincere. Our ambition is to make TBWA one of the most interesting places to be in the industry. And we are trying hard every day to get there.

We began by concentrating on the basics, on what we do best, focusing on what in our network is now known as Disruption. We have been applying our method to all of the brands with which we have been entrusted, resulting in varying degrees of transformation for not just Nissan, Adidas, Pedigree, PlayStation, Absolut, Mars, Chivas, and Nivea, but for the vast majority of our brands around the world.

We then went on to invent, hone, and develop our skills in five areas: organization, integration, business plans, new business, and internal communication. We fixed a precise course of action regarding each of these activities, which I am about to describe. We have our own ways of seeing and doing things. They are not always conventional, and they are based on a set of strong convictions.

ORGANIZATION

Imagine you work for Procter & Gamble, in charge of Pampers in France. For whatever reason, you come to the conclusion that the French advertising campaign needs to be changed. All things considered, which of your two bosses should be the final decision maker: the president of the French operation, or the worldwide manager of the Pampers brand? The first is naturally concerned, because the decisions taken will have a direct effect on his bottom line. But since the president manages several different product lines, from diapers to soap powders, from beauty products to perfumes, he or she will never hope to reach the level of expertise on the brand as will the worldwide brand manager. This person is likely to have a more precise grasp of the situation, having accumulated experience in only one category, but in over one hundred countries.

The reality is that there needs to be a joint decision, using a matrix system. Each global company has developed its own approach. Each seeks to find its own balance between local and global, defining its system according to its history, culture, and sector of activity. Some of our clients have developed more elaborate systems, such as Nissan, which has a three-way matrix system, comprised of regional poles, worldwide product programs, and, at the top, cross-functional teams. You cannot avoid defining your own matrix, and those who pretend otherwise are quickly proven wrong.

For our part, we have developed a very clear-cut organization. We have kept the inherently necessary regional management structures. This means we have managers for America, Asia, Europe, Africa, and the Middle East.

Along with this, we have strengthened our global account directors' authority. The global account leaders for Apple in Los Angeles, Nivea in Hamburg, and Absolut in New York, for example, have complete power. They can decide to modify a strategy or campaign on the other side of the world. They even have the authority to request the replacement, if they deem necessary, of a local account director. Global client management is totally centralized, even if this is not always to everyone's liking.

This is all classic stuff. What deserves to be emphasized is our way of integrating disciplines with geographies. To make the alternative clear and our choice understandable, I often give a counter example. Back in the 1970s, when Lester Wunderman accepted Ed Ney's offer to make Wunderman the Young & Rubicam group's direct marketing brand, it was on the condition that Wunderman would be a separate profit center. I was at Young & Rubicam at the time. This decision resulted in a lack of synergy, with very few clients shared between Young & Rubicam and Wunderman.

For me, this was a mistake.

This way of working has since been followed by most marketing service networks, each wanting to operate independently within large global holding companies. Direct marketing people want to stay with direct marketing people, interactive specialists with interactive specialists, and agency creative people with agency creatives. They understand each other better that way. The problem is that they stick together, in isolated silos.

We have adopted a completely opposite type of system, totally decentralizing the management of disciplines. The heads of our direct marketing arm at, for example, Tequila in London or Shanghai report directly to the presidents of the United Kingdom and Chinese groups and only indirectly, with a dotted line, to the network president of Tequila Worldwide. For us, successful integration relies on close collaboration, familiarity among the numerous parties involved—in short, on proximity. We believe the benefit of proximity outweighs the merits of a more centralized organization.

Matrix systems blend interests that are diverse, even diverging, but not contradictory. Generally speaking, several systems are possible. And so one must be decided on, often the one which comes with the least potentially restrictive disadvantages. Then, after the choice is made, you must stick with it. Nothing is more costly, both financially and commercially, than flitting back and forth, indulging in procrastination and indecision.

We are in a privileged position to observe our clients' behavior and notice that some lack rigor in managing matrix systems, or perhaps have a deliberate desire to tolerate ambiguity, perhaps even encourage it. This situation exists because some executives still believe in managing people and decisions politically, and others cultivate ambiguities to create what they call "healthy tensions." I do not believe in any of this in the slightest.

For this reason, we have implemented a two-tier system, very centralized in terms of client management but totally decentralized in the management of disciplines. Though its inherent relevance can be debated, there is no denying its precision.

INTEGRATION

Today our competitors are organized, like us, into groups, made up of companies specialized in digital marketing, public relations, events, entertainment, retail activation, and advertising. Each group has adopted a multidisciplinary model.

Our French group alone comprises over twenty companies, each with its own discipline. Our fashion PR agency organizes shows for prestigious brands such as Christian Dior, Jean-Paul Gaultier, Yves Saint Laurent, Kenzo, and Louis Vuitton. Our custom publishing arm produces weekly the equivalent of three newsmagazines, thanks to the efforts of the hundreds of journalists it employs. Our "nonprofit" division works with over twenty nongovernmental organizations on a daily basis, such as Médecins du Monde and the Red Cross. Our digital publishing company has invented software that allows us to reproduce catalog photos of cars that have not even been built yet. Our events management agency staged the hundred-year anniversary celebrations of the Tour de France on the Champs-Élysées, installed a real locomotive on the sidewalks of Wall Street to mark Alstom's listing on the stock market, and created the Absolut Metropolis exhibition that has toured the world's modern art museums.

The challenge consists in encouraging each of these specialized companies to work together in harmony. Over time, we have gained a more than ample understanding of the subject, and written it down in authentic tablets of stone. In a meeting that took place in Seville six years ago, the chairman of the French group presented the Ten Commandments of Integration. These rules are an integral part of the TBWA's culture, and there should be no exceptions to them.

Rule number one: The word "subsidiary" has been banished. We only ever refer to our "sister companies" or "partner companies."

Rule number two: Representatives from all disciplines concerned participate in the client briefing; everyone must be treated at an equal level.

Rule number three: "Finders' fees" between agencies are strictly forbidden. Everyone must help each other on the basis that the help given and received will balance out over time. If it does not, the chances are that one of our companies is not competitive enough, and then it is time for action . . .

Many times new recruits from other agencies have asked me how our finders' fees operate between our group companies. They are always surprised, thinking I have misunderstood the question, when I tell them that this practice does not exist within our organization.

Seven other rules of this type shape our group's character. The underlying idea is to strengthen our partnerships on equal terms. The majority of our competitors talk about this commitment, but they infringe on it on a daily basis. For us, disobeying these rules is one of the biggest mistakes one of our executives can make. Harmony relies on a fragile balance.

Perhaps the most unexpected rule is that account directors are never *forced* to work with our own group companies. An agency director can choose to work with an outside direct marketing company for a particular client. A PR executive is not obliged to work with our advertising agency to create a corporate campaign, if he thinks he can find a more appropriate solution elsewhere. But over time, our group companies learn to appreciate one another and choose to work together of their own accord. And this leads to much better effectiveness.

ACTION PLANS

American management books on corporate strategy fill entire aisles in the bookstores in New York. I flick through them occasionally, picking up opinions and various analyses of concepts such as "core competencies," "sense of purpose," "value migration," and so on. More often than not, the authors of these books are discussing how to build "long-term strategic plans."

To be honest, I am not much of a believer in these all-embracing strategic plans, which tend to be spread over three years or more. It is hazardous to establish a strategy on the basis of predictions. The key is to be prepared, to put yourself into a situation whereby you are ready to reply to any challenge and quick to react.

This is why our business plans are different from those of other companies. They do not describe strategies or objectives in any way. They simply outline the tasks that need to be accomplished.

David Maister, the Harvard professor to whom we already referred, made an astute observation about this:

> Much of what professional firms do in the name of strategic planning is a complete waste of time, no more effective than individuals making New Year's resolutions. The reasons are the same in both situations. Personally and professionally, we already know what we should do: lose weight, give up smoking and exercise more. In business, strategic plans are also stuffed with familiar goals: build client relationships, act like team players and provide fulfilling, motivating careers. We want the benefits of these things. We know what to do, we know why we should do it and we know how to do it. Yet most of us don't change, as individuals or as businesses.

These kinds of observations have led us to develop action plans that are very concrete. They are condensed into what we call the *15-Actions Plan*. Each of the five chapters that make up each plan—Creative Product, Disruption, Connections, Talents, and Organic Growth—has an average of three actions. The plan involves putting to paper fifteen actions or tasks—not vague objectives—that the managers of each of our agencies must commit themselves to accomplishing within the year. The plans are reviewed every quarter. Perhaps you are president of a direct marketing company with no number two. In November you vow to recruit your successor. It is not so important if you have made no progress by March. In June you can still get away with it, but by September you will definitely be on thin ice.

I would like to be sure that we build and follow-up on plans very thoroughly in each of our offices. The *15-Actions Plan* speeds up decision making by one or two quarters. Do the math: 15 actions multiplied by 238 companies add up to making four thousand decisions faster.

It is hard not to believe that this does contribute to generating at least one or two more points of organic growth at a global level.

NEW BUSINESS

Agencies need to win new clients in order to survive. Acquiring this new business leads to Homeric battles. There can only ever be one winner; there is no difference between second or last place. An agency that consistently comes in second would be not far from being the best in the world, but it would go out of business.

In a new-business presentation, you usually have around ninety minutes to convince, persuade, and conquer. These are the most costly ninety minutes imaginable. The amount of time and money spent on their preparation can reach colossal proportions. Winning is all that counts.

To win, you have to blow your competitors out of the water. Complacency is a fatal error. We cannot afford to underestimate our adversaries. The majority of the time, one of the competitors will perform outstandingly and will win by "a few inches," to use the words of Al Pacino in *Any Given Sunday*. In this Oliver Stone film, Pacino plays Tony d'Amato, the charismatic football coach. The prematch pep talk becomes a defining moment. Leaning against the changing-room lockers, Pacino wells up with passion and gives the speech that all coaches dream of giving once in their lives:

> "You find out life's this game of inches. And so is football. Because in either game, life or football, the margin for error is so small. I mean . . . one half a step

too late or too early and you don't quite make it. One half second too slow or too fast, you don't quite catch it. The inches we need are everywhere around us. They are in every break of the game, every minute, every second."

I have taken part in hundreds of new-business meetings. They are the moments of truth in the advertising industry. Tensions always run high. Hundreds of hours of work have been put in, hundreds of thousands of dollars spent. In the run-up, content has been discussed, dissected, pulled apart over several long days and nights, and everything hinges on your final performance.

As soon as the prospect, the potential client, enters the meeting room, he or she becomes a spectator. The theatrics—which is no exaggerated term—have been meticulously tuned. Everything is dramatized. We rehearse several times, but we only go on stage once. There are only premieres in our profession, which is a pity. Some presentations would be good enough to continue their run in public for a week.

I enjoy the tension, the anxiety of these meetings: the heavy atmosphere, the forced smiles. For fear of making a mistake, I always memorize my speeches. Once, during a pitch for the Printemps department store account, I had to remember the names of over ten designers I had never heard of . . . Visual aids, slides, PowerPoint presentations all need to be perfect. One single error, one spelling mistake, risks giving the impression of last-minute preparation and will affect client confidence. The whole ritual hinges on a series of minor details.

Perhaps Bertrand Delanoë, mayor of Paris, has never seen *Any Given Sunday*. A city's Olympic bid is like a new-business pitch on a very different scale. There is no bronze or silver medal, only the gold. The Baron de Coubertin, inventor of the modern Olympic Games, said: "What is important is to participate." Winning for him was less important. This is not the case, however, when a city is pitching for the Olympics. It is not about participating, it is only about winning. The Paris bid fell into practically every trap we have learned to recognize: talking about yourself more than the prospective client, refusing to face up to your potential weaknesses, failing to choose the best pre-senters, going over the same turf from meeting to meeting without ever bringing in something new, and, above all, succumbing to "wishful thinking," new business's worst enemy.

The presentation to the Olympic Committee held no surprises. The French team performed predictably, no more, no less. It showed people what they were expecting to see.

A host of other reasons go toward explaining Paris's failure to win the Games. For example, I remember feeling anxious when I discov-ered that Sir Sebastian Coe had charged Michael J. Power, former global business services officer at Procter & Gamble, with supervising the United Kingdom's presentation film. The English had no doubt understood that they needed to avoid falling into the "talking-about-yourself trap." Power would remind them of this, drawing from his experience.

In the first ranks of the French delegation, public administrators and civil servants were highly represented, with only a small number of athletes present. On the British side, the ranks were made up exclusively of athletes. Paris talked Paris, while London talked Olympics. Al Pacino was right. Paris finished two inches short—two votes on this occasion.

Paradoxically, going into the meeting, Paris was in a less enviable position than people thought. In everybody's mind, the "City of Light" was the front-runner. In this sort of situation, it is actually rare to win. The reason is simple. When we concentrate on building on our already acknowledged strengths, we stop surprising, we invent nothing new. We repeat rather than amaze, at the same time as the competition, aware of being behind, will stake its all. Two or three competitors will have nothing to lose in taking risks. More often than not, one of them will exceed expectations.

An obsession with winning needs to be behind every new-business drive. It is better to win and be wrong than be right and lose. In the first instance you have weeks or months to put things right, in the second you end up without the client and will never have the opportunity to be right.

This way of stating the issue—being right or winning—has nothing to do with cynicism. I am not suggesting under any circumstances that it is legitimate to win at all costs, or by any means. Hopefully, our agency's past integrity should illustrate that we have always known where to draw the line when it comes to new business.

Our job is about helping our clients go further, making them discover the opportunities available to them through creativity and risk-taking. Some come round slowly, others after only a few meetings. It always takes more than one. I remember an innovative campaign idea we presented in Paris to the Printemps department store around the theme *Encounter Emotion*. At the time, the most dynamic department stores in the world were Seibu and Parco in Tokyo. We studied their advertising campaigns over a period of six months, preparing ourselves, more or less consciously, to adopt a "Japanese" style of advertising, a style that was certainly unexpected, not to say controversial. The Printemps executive committee unanimously bought the campaign after only a few minutes of discussion. Although the chairman of Printemps at the time and the other members of the executive committee were not far from being our most conservative clients, we had worked closely with them over a six-month period so that they could discover progressively the hidden strength of Japanese advertising. This half-year preparation would obviously have been impossible within the limited time of a new-business pitch.

In the same way, I no longer believe in these grand performances in which agencies overemphatically sell their campaigns to clients. It no longer works this way. The large majority of our campaigns, and especially the most creative ones, could never have existed without our clients' contribution. This is true not only because the clients actually approved the campaigns, but because their thinking, intuition, comments, and often ideas have been instrumental to the agency's creative work.

Consequently, in new business we allow ourselves to hold back our most provocative, or even our most impactful, work in order to be able to come with it later. I know it is surprising, but I believe the famous iPod "silhouettes" campaign, with shadows dancing against colored backgrounds, would probably not have made it through one round of a new-business pitch. It is astoundingly simple, and this is always disconcerting at first glance.

In order to win, the objective is simple: Make it hard, even impossible, for the prospect to choose another agency. Make us the only possible solution. We have been trying to achieve this from the beginning in 1984, back when we were BDDP. We became French new-business champions that year thanks to wins with Michelin, McDonald's, and BMW. Not bad for a young new agency. We had already understood that new business is more about rigor than inspiration. Acquiring new clients requires both a systematic and a comprehensive approach.

We developed what we called the "principles of new business," and forbade ourselves ever to diverge from this ever-evolving list.

Here are some of the principles: One of them concerns the signals your physical location sends out. When the client first walks into the building, he must get the impression of a clean, bright, friendly place, with a sense of vibrancy, not a gloomy, untidy place where he feels unwanted. In the words of Head & Shoulders, *You never get a second chance to make a first impression.* It is a matter of common sense. Yet many agencies are guilty of overlooking this fact.

Speaking of untidy places, this reminds me of a famous story from London. A prestigious potential client—the chairman of one of the biggest companies in Britain—presents himself at an agency's reception. The receptionist's desk is empty. The visitor waits for ten minutes before someone approaches him and asks him quite rudely what he is doing there. He has sat down in the meantime on a worn-out couch, his feet resting on a threadbare carpet. The tables are full of dirty coffee cups, the ashtray of foul-smelling cigarette butts. The moment the visitor gets up to leave in frustration, the agency chairman approaches him. Well aware of his guest's annoyance (as it is he who has orchestrated the entire scenario), he says: "I'm sorry, sir, I just wanted you to experience for yourself what we feel like when we use your service." The prospective client was none other than the chairman of British Rail, which was well known at the time for the mediocrity of its equipment and services. The agency, Allen Brady and Marsh, won the business.

A few weeks after the merger of our companies, I attended a new-business meeting in New York. I overheard Laurie Coots, now our worldwide chief marketing officer, remind one of her colleagues to respect the one-meeting-ahead rule. I was surprised to hear this in another agency, the agency we had just been merged with. This was one of the first principles we had always tried to instill into the minds of our employees in Europe. Laurie reminded me that almost fifteen years earlier, Jay Chiat had invited me to present our new-business methods to his troops in California. We had achieved such a high conversion rate that our reputation had spread as far as Los Angeles. Laurie was a young assistant at that time. She adopted our principles from that day forward, principles that have stood the test of time.

Why "one meeting ahead"? Because we want to be one step ahead in our discussions with prospective clients.

A classic pitch is in three stages. The first is the agency introduction. At this introductory stage, our method is to take only 20 percent of the time allotted to showing our credentials and talk about ourselves, and to use the remaining 80 percent to ask questions. Even if the prospect's problem appears to be infinitely complex, it is never difficult to come to the meeting armed with a list of relevant questions. This has a dual effect: It gets us through to the second round and gives us a clearer picture of what the briefing will involve.

Before the second meeting, where the client will brief us, we already start working on advertising strategies, concepts, embryonic campaign ideas. By doing this, our questions at this meeting will be guided by work that has already begun. Rather than being mere additional information, the answers our prospective clients give us provide insight into the relevance of our approaches.

This puts us one step ahead of the competition. And one step is often a decisive advantage. Remember Al Pacino . . .

Another of our principles is to avoid the temptation to be "fair." Those who are best at putting together presentations are not necessarily the best at presenting them. In the words of Nick Baum, head of our

Western European network, and somewhat of an expert on the subject: "There is no indication that Shakespeare was a brilliant actor, or that Richard Burton could have written a convincing Hamlet." The decisions that must be taken may seem unfair, even brutal. But people need to realize that the reward does not lie in attending these new-business presentations. There are other ways of acknowledging a job well done.

The next principle is perhaps the most important of all. In thirty years of new business, I have not seen one rehearsal that has not led to major improvements in the presentation, such as changes in rhythm, the balancing of arguments, or even resulting in us starting all over again. You must convince participants to rehearse "for real." Last-minute rehearsals, point checks in the elevator on the way to the presentation room, must be avoided at all costs. Sometimes it has taken us years to have the opportunity to pitch to a particular prospect. This will have led to a countless number of people having spent so many weeks working toward the final presentation, often day and night. Last-minute improvisation is a fatal mistake and an act of gross irresponsibility. I remember the words of heavyweight champion Joe Frazier: "If you've cheated in the dark of morning—you're getting found out under the bright lights."

We follow over thirty principles in this way, with the knowledge that if we apply them all to the letter, our conversion rate will be over 50 percent. And we also know that if we do not, the rate could quickly fall to zero. When we lose, very often I know the reason why. This is where our reputation for intransigence comes from, as we will not settle for situations where only 90 percent of the criteria have been respected.

"The client says no, let the sale commence" goes the old sales rep adage, a remark that reflects the buyer's unease. It is always easier to refuse than to accept. The buyer feels insecure, threatened, exposed, skeptical, concerned, suspicious. Anything but positive. The majority of our principles are designed to make the prospective client comfortable. For example, I always try to present our creative work as early on as possible, although most of our competitors present it at the end, as a sort of climax, a grand finale. The wait can be very frustrating for the client.

"Beware of these presentations when you talk for one hour about what the prospect is going to see, explaining how great it is going to be, and all the characteristics the campaigns will have," I once told the agency. And I added: "You promise a lot. The clients' imaginations are fueled. And when they see the end result, it's very different from what they imagined. And it won't always be a good surprise. So try to show the ads early in the meeting and, as I said, spend more time defending the qualities of the campaign after the prospect has seen it than before." One day a client gave us only one hour to present. I remember presenting our creative work after only seven minutes—a personal record, I might add. We often forget the evident fact that it is easier to sell something people have already seen than the contrary. When the prospect already knows a campaign, the arguments in its favor become more obvious. It is a question of common sense, a sense that is unfortunately not very commonly found.

Anyway, why wait? Why not put an end to these tedious meetings in which we put clients to sleep for half an hour, even an hour, with our so-called intelligent observations? The only real purpose of these endless minutes is to reassure the people presenting. It gives them a feeling like taking a deep breath before taking the plunge. It is better to dive straight in.

New business is the agency's lifeblood. It is obviously a key factor in its growth. It is also the gauge of the agency's competitiveness and consequently its morale. New business is like a mirror; it shows us a reflection of who we are that can sometimes be cruel, but is always accurate.

Therefore, new-business activity must be at the core of the agency. To win, we should never leave anything to chance. We should never forget that, especially in new business, "hope is not a strategy."

Some say that you need to be lucky in new business. And they may be right. Napoleon said he only wanted "lucky generals." But I prefer the point of view of Gary Player, winner of nine golf majors. He was interviewed by a journalist after winning one of them, thanks to some very long putts on the final holes. The journalist congratulated Player but could not resist saying how lucky he had been at the end of the game. Gary Player, polite as ever, replied: "Yes, I was lucky, but it's a funny thing . . . I find that the harder I practice, the luckier I get!"

INTERNAL COMMUNICATION

In many companies, the chief executive addresses employees only once a year, and even then, in an indirect manner, through the year-end review. This vision of the company is obsolete. The company of today is an ever-changing entity, with assets that are more and more volatile and growth that is increasingly unstable.

We needed to adopt a different kind of rhythm. To be able to spread our culture, I decided to write a weekly newsletter and distribute it to all employees. I call it a memo, though in style it is much closer to a newspaper editorial.

After the first three or four memos, a colleague from the BDDP era took me aside when I was on a trip to Paris. He said that this way of communicating was not like me at all and that, for him, it was a by-product of old-school paternalism. Somewhat disheartened, I carried on regardless. I am glad I did because these short texts, which we have called "Thursdays" after the day they are sent out, have contributed to weaving our current group culture. They tighten the threads of our network.

By now I have sent more than three hundred of them, and each has provoked its weekly hour of worry for me. I use them to address various subjects relating to the network, its employees, its clients, the awards we receive, and so on.

From one Thursday to the next, I may talk about Nissan's turnaround by Carlos Ghosn; the values of transparency at TBWA; the link between employee and client satisfaction; the life of Jay Chiat, founder of Chiat/Day; the year's best management books; the campaign for the Korean soccer team at the previous World Cup; the oldest client in the network (a department store in Mexico); some new Disruption tools; our opinion on the anti-advertising book *No Logo* by Naomi Klein; the launch of the euro; "open day" weekends at our Paris agency (for students from top universities); the brand voted by the press as the most influential in the world (Apple).

I also cover TBWA training seminars; the episode of *Sex and the City* in which the Absolut bottle plays the leading role; the architecture of our Shanghai office; a tribute to Nicole Cooper, my assistant for twenty-three years; the alarming power of the TiVo digital recorder; The Cannes "Agency of the Year" title awarded to TBWA\Paris three years running; Disruption in India; our Skittles win and the subsequent Snickers win two years later; La Mode en Images (Fashion in images), our French unit that organizes dozens of fashion shows; the number-one rank of our agency in Finland and the number-two rank of our agency in South Africa; criticism of the jargon used in the agency and marketing world; the Venice Biennial; a celebration of our election as best Asian network; Sony in 2005, and then Adidas in 2006, being named "Advertiser of the Year"; Steve Jobs's speech to Stanford students; the joint venture in Japan between TBWA and Hakuhodo; the fear of dealing with what is already being called post-globalization . . .

I have gone on to write memos on Kuwait, Egypt, Lebanon, Arabian inventiveness and its influence on the cultural development of the West. I never miss the opportunity to share information that can bring people closer. This all goes toward creating a common culture. These letters are read every Thursday morning, from Tokyo to Los Angeles, and are usually displayed somewhere in the agency. Some of our clients have even asked to be put on the mailing list.

I have chosen to print here three that give a good idea of the diversity of subjects covered. The first is dedicated to one of our agencies, TBWA\Hunt\Lascaris in South Africa, the second to one of our clients, Carlos Ghosn, now chief executive of Nissan and Renault, and the third to one of the brands we manage to the envy of those around us, Sony PlayStation. An agency, a client, a brand.

Twenty years ago, when apartheid was rife, who could have imagined that South Africa would go on to become the Rainbow Nation? Convention had it that this country would remain in black and white forever.

John Hunt and Reg Lascaris founded their agency in 1983. Ranked second in turnover, it is the most creative agency in the country by far. The agency owes part of its rise to its long-time association with Nelson Mandela. John and Reg were behind the campaigns for the first democratic election in the country as well as for the new constitution. Their first African National Congress campaign was launched in 1991. They had already been campaigning for some time against apartheid and for a more open society. The fact that they were not Afrikaaners acted in their favor. John was born in Rhodesia, now Zimbabwe, and Reg has Greek origins. The duo published *The South African Dream*, a best-seller that insists, without arrogance, that South Africa is in a fighting position to save Africa. As they say, "If Africa dies, the world dies with it."

I have written several weekly newsletters on this agency, which without a doubt represents the very best of TBWA. This was one of them:

In line with the country's ten years of democracy celebrations, the Financial Mail decided to award an agency the accolade of "Agency of the Decade"—the agency that's made the biggest contribution to the advertising industry during the first ten years of democracy. TBWA\ Hunt\Lascaris has won this award, and here are the key moments that punctuated this decade:

1994: They were chosen as the agency for the first ever Democratic Election and for Nelson Mandela.

1995: They worked on a campaign to introduce the new Constitution.

1996: Business Against Crime (BAC) was created in response to high crime levels. They did the campaign.

1997: They worked on a national campaign with the aim of normalizing governance (Masakhane). They also launched the Tax Amnesty campaign.

1998: They launched the "Arrive Alive" road safety campaign.

1999: They ran the second election campaign for Thabo Mbeki (the current South African president).

2000: They worked on the first initiative to encourage South Africans to embrace tourism, "The Welcome" campaign.

2001: They launched the first AIDS Prevention campaign.

2002: They launched "The Proudly South African" campaign.

2004: They were re-appointed to fight the battle against AIDS.

To conclude the memo, I reproduced the text the agency had crafted to celebrate the new democracy in South Africa:

> Because we dance when we're happy
>
> Because we dance when we're sad
>
> Because we now live side by side like we've been doing it for years
>
> Because our past is as bad as our future is good
>
> Because "ja well no fine" makes sense to us
>
> Because we say sharp!
>
> Because you're never too old to graduate
>
> Because the streets are our malls
>
> And the trees are our temples
>
> Because we speak eleven tongues
>
> Yet we fly one flag.

These phrases have become the hymn of the national airline company, South African Airways. And as for TBWA\Hunt\Lascaris, it was not only the agency of the decade. In another vote, it was quite simply named "Agency of the Century."

Our two best-known clients are probably Steve Jobs and Carlos Ghosn. Each has come up against the same pronounced skepticism.

When Steve Jobs returned to Apple in 1997, Michael Dell declared that it would be wiser for the company to file for bankruptcy: "What would I do if I was managing Apple? I'd shut it down and give the money back to the shareholders." Bob Lutz, current vice chairman of General Motors, put things even more bluntly when he was asked for his opinion on Renault's decision to come to Nissan's aid: "You would be just as well putting five billion dollars in a container and throwing it out into the middle of the ocean."

I have already spoken and will speak again later of Steve Jobs. As for Carlos Ghosn, we are all familiar with the extraordinary turnaround he has achieved for Nissan. The Japanese automobile manufacturer has performed a veritable renaissance, with the new chief executive saying some years later: "Purgatory isn't so bad when you're coming from hell." The Nissan chief executive needed a great number of qualities to be able to orchestrate the journey with such prowess. Among them I would gladly highlight his talent for bringing together people with different origins and disciplines and getting them to work together, an exercise that may often be grueling but always produces positive results. Most companies are really only "multinational"; in other words, a simple addition of nationalities, which is the very opposite of being multicultural. In one of my Thursdays, I borrowed from the speech Ghosn gave on diversity at the New York Japan Society annual dinner:

> You do not learn much from people who are exactly like you. You learn the most from interacting with people whose makeup is different from your own—from people with a different background . . . age . . . language . . . education . . . or social experience. We have found it to be true at Nissan. In the past, engineers only talked to engineers. Designers talked to designers. The Japanese preferred to deal with the

Japanese, the Americans with Americans, and so on. One of the first things we did at the start of Nissan's revival was to tear down some of the walls that separated functions and regions ... In this century, globalization is an indisputable fact due to technology and to information and capital flow. The challenge is to use differences to learn and grow while reinforcing your own identity. Keep your roots while opening the door to constructive, progressive change ...

For Carlos Ghosn, the only viable management is management without boundaries. I have heard him speak on the subjects of diversity and multiculturalism on several occasions, issues he holds especially close to his heart. Openness toward other cultures is the key to effectiveness and the success of his cross-functional teams is the proof. At the same time, I can feel his emotion when he speaks about diversity. Born in Brazil, having studied in France and worked in France, Brazil, the United States, and Japan, he is a genuine "world citizen," to quote the title of the book he published in France in 2003.

Isaac Newton noticed that many more men build walls than bridges. Carlos Ghosn is a builder of bridges.

I dream of managing an agency made up of ten thousand world citizens. Not stateless individuals without roots, but rather ten thousand employees who are proud of their origins, passionate about their culture, and keen to preserve their differences. Ten thousand people who at the same time take real enjoyment in working together without barriers. There is nothing more satisfying than seeing a Californian and a Thai coming up with a solution together for a Chinese. Our culture allows this to happen every single day in our agency. And my role is to increase the frequency of these "accidents."

The third weekly newsletter I would like to mention concerns Hollywood and PlayStation. Hollywood is the heart of the entertainment industry, and has been for almost a century. It appeared invincible. And yet, as I wrote in the following lines back in 2002, revolutionary products are capable of overturning the established order:

> In a survey, people were asked if their PlayStation experience compared favorably with the movies. 59% answered yes. So it's no surprise that, today, the gaming industry has already surpassed the movie industry in terms of sales. Who could have foreseen such an outcome only 10 years ago? Who could have ever imagined that gaming would outgrow Hollywood?
>
> More on the comparison between games and movies: Kaz Hirai, President of Sony PlayStation, was ranked as the fourth most powerful person in the entertainment industry by *Entertainment Weekly*. This is the first time anyone from the gaming industry made it on to the list. Kaz outranked the likes of Steven Spielberg, David Geffen and Jeffrey Katzenberg from Dreamworks, rapper Eminem, director Ridley Scott, media queen Oprah Winfrey, and actor George Clooney.

A great number of the campaigns we have produced for Sony PlayStation have been recognized with awards, leading Sony PlayStation to be named "Advertiser of the Year" at the 2005 Cannes Festival. At the ceremony, PlayStation's inventor, Ken Kutaragi, stated that the advertising produced for the brand over the last ten years had been particularly inspiring.

But what pleases us the most when it comes to Sony can be found outside of these campaigns, which, however outstanding, still represent a conventional communications approach. Contrary to expectations, what we are most proud of lies outside of the media: The launch of the PS1 started off virally. As I have discussed, we sparked off an irresistible word-of-mouth effect and made millions of adolescents feel that they were part of a movement. The first phase of media advertising surfaced six months after the launch . . . Today an increasing number of seminars and conferences are held to describe product launches that have been successful without recourse to traditional media. People react as if the speakers have discovered a completely new discipline, as if they are messiahs. The launch of the PS1 dates back to 1996. PlayStation was clearly very ahead of its time.

And since then, the tradition has been perpetuated. For the recent launch of the PS3, as with the PS2 before it, Sony called upon viral marketing, always starting with a series of unexpected events on the Net.

I have written hundreds of other memos, on subjects so diverse that these memos may appear random. I have imagined how Disruption might present itself in the financial world; I have given the recipes from our so-called *Cookbook*, a three-hundred-page book written by Fiona Clancy that outlines each of Disruption's tools and how to use them; I have stood up against economic patriotism, yet another "French disease"; I have condemned the arrogance of so many people in advertising, adding that I have always been won over by job candidates who are 100 percent confident and 0 percent pretentious, because they are always the ones to succeed.

I have also covered "Room 13," an initiative we have taken to help underprivileged children from impoverished areas, from Scotland to South Africa, to escape the rigors of their daily lives. We have provided them with means, and not just financial, since we also recruit art teachers, thus giving them access to creative activities, such as painting or sculpture. I wrote another Thursday to describe a show of their work in Johannesburg and the BBC documentary devoted to them.

In February 2003 I announced the birth of the Disruption Grand Prix, our internal festival that takes place every year at the same time as the Cannes advertising festival. Only a few weeks after this announcement, I was delighted to see our first award going to our Korean agency for a campaign it created around the 2002 soccer World Cup. There are relatively few English-speakers in our Seoul agency. But we had no need for explanations. Big ideas are universal.

The weekly newsletter I send to the network is just one of several initiatives that allow us to communicate with each other. The idea of the chief executive communicating "one way," top-down to his troops, is already a concept belonging to another age. New technology has provided each of our employees with the opportunity to communicate with the entire network.

As I write, we have launched our newest intranet, the first of the Web 2.0 generation. We have named it *mytbwa.com*. It is not an evolved version of our previous intranet, *insideTBWA*, but a total revolution. We believe that companies today need to increase the sharing of information, not its control. We have purely and simply deleted our existing intranet to start from scratch and created an intranet based on the Wikipedia model, relying exclusively on user contributions.

Each communications discipline and each TBWA brand has its own channel, rather like a television channel. Animated by chief editors and contributors from our entire workforce across the world, each channel serves as a blog. Relevant pieces of information and comments are enriched by "wiki"-style functions, allowing us all to contribute and download the best additions.

It is constantly updated from every computer, BlackBerry, or telephone. It is even possible to download spots or podcasts onto an iPod.

This approach is going to have a profound effect on the sharing of knowledge. We are already working on the next version, which will allow our clients to access this live information and enrich it. Internal communication will no longer be aimed exclusively toward the interior; it will simply become *communication*.

* * *

As I have said, our corporate values are not particularly original in their own right. Rather, it is our relentless determination to defend them that creates the difference.

In the same way, whatever we do, whether it concerns our organization, our way of building action plans, winning new clients, or communicating, we have given ourselves a precise course of action. And we are not wavering.

8

Principles

(Or How a Culture Can Foster Principles that Go against Convention)

Called on to succeed his father to the throne, Prince T'ai went out to listen to the teachings of the Great Master Pan Ku. No sooner had he arrived than he was sent out into the forest of Ming-Li. One year later Pan Ku asked him what he had heard in the forest. The prince evoked the singing of birds, the rustling of leaves, and the whistling of the wind . . . The master sent him back into the forest. On his return, T'ai explained to Pan Ku that after listening for days and nights, he had started to hear the inaudible: the singing of budding flowers, the whispering of the sun, the murmuring of the dew . . .

The master answered approvingly: "The ability to hear the inaudible is a necessary quality to become a good leader. If a leader has learned how to listen closely to his people's hearts, to pay attention to the feelings they do not dare speak of, to their unexpressed pain and their hidden grief, then he can inspire confidence, understand when things are wrong, and quickly discover his subjects' needs."

During the early days of 2006, I found myself facing a sea of mostly exceptional students. The fable I had just recited to them was called "The Noise of the Forest." I had borrowed it from W. Chan Kim and Renée Maubourgne, two INSEAD professors who had published an article on leadership in the *Harvard Business Review* and illustrated their points with Korean apologues. Since then they have published the international best-seller *Blue Ocean Strategies*.

I was back on the HEC campus, where I myself had studied, having accepted an invitation from Valérie Gauthier to come and talk about leadership. I had hesitated to accept this invitation, finding it hard to imagine myself giving lessons. Valérie insisted, convinced that, in my over thirty-year career, during which time I had worked in many different fields, I would have met and been able to closely observe many leaders, which is true. I have been a privileged witness, observing success and failure close-up. I have sensed the tension within management committees, and I have felt the hesitations of the greatest among them, and the others. Like all agency executives, I have also advised some of them on a more personal level.

Most of the students were between the ages of twenty-five and thirty, and they came from all walks of life. It was a more mature audience than I had expected. For example, I remember one Romanian student who had campaigned against the Ilescu government and a Chinese student who was a specialist in bilateral Sino-Japanese relations.

Oriental wisdom is full of parables, which can add an unexpected depth to our perception. Several others were reproduced in the *Harvard Business Review* article, such as "The Wisdom of the Mountains" and "The Wheel and the Light." They all had one thing in common: The student did not understand right away and would be sent back into the mountains or the forest several times by the master before gradually acquiring a higher level of sensitivity and a better understanding of the world for himself.

These fables show that personal growth comes through an unending series of experiences and challenges. Just like their authors, I do not believe much in natural leadership. The majority of chief executives I know were not necessarily destined for that path. They have been molded by the events they have lived through and the people they have met. Which is not to say that everything comes naturally and without effort, just that we ourselves influence these events and personally choose most of the people who will be important to us in our lives. One day we find ourselves in the right place at the right time. This never really happens by chance. The person in the right place may say he has been lucky, but deep down, he knows how much getting there has cost in terms of effort and patience.

It took an outsider to IBM by the name of Lou Gerstner to turn the computer electronics giant around. Renault was lucky enough to have a senior civil servant, Louis Schweitzer, at the helm when it was privatized and then was fortunate to welcome a world citizen, Carlos Ghosn, as his successor. Crowned by his striking success at Nissan, Ghosn would go on to open the company doors wide to globalization, catapulting it definitively into the modern world.

I could give numerous other examples of where a person has appeared heaven-sent, the timing is so perfect. For example, Steve Jobs was the only person who could have saved the company he had created when it was on the brink of collapse.

The concept of leadership thus evolves into a much narrower question: How can you make sure you will be in the right place at the right time? I answered this question by saying that it is important not to blindly follow established principles, again recommending the avoidance of "well-trodden paths," and not to be content with the standard advice given by so many so-called specialists.

I suggested to the students that they should not wait ten or twenty years before adopting principles of their own. I also advised them to act as vagabonds, moving from one position to another in the first few years in order to avoid making the fatal mistake of not being in a job they liked. And I offered them a range of seemingly unorthodox advice, a set of *counterprinciples*.

As I will show, these counterprinciples create a different kind of practice, a different way of managing, and a way of seeing the company that is particular to us. They participate in fashioning our culture just as much as everything I have already mentioned.

FIRST CONVICTIONS

It appears obvious that wisdom, or at the very least discernment, comes with age. Having said this, I believe one should forge principles as early as possible on how to behave in one's professional life. These will serve as milestones, observation posts, all along the way. They will constitute benchmarks to refer to in times of hesitation and difficult decisions.

I recommended to the students that they rapidly form their own set of convictions, that they choose principles, and stick to them faithfully, even rigidly if necessary. As an example, I explained mine and ours.

Our first conviction is that you should invest in your strengths. My first boss was an American named Rolf. He explained to me in my very first working weeks the differences in approaches between Procter & Gamble and Colgate. If a P&G product had a 12 percent market share in Normandy and only 6 percent in Alsace, P&G would spend twice as much in Normandy as in Alsace. P&G invests where it is strong. Colgate would have done the opposite, believing that the 6 percent in Alsace, lower than the national average, was clear evidence of underexploited potential requiring investment. For obvious economic reasons, the two approaches are irreconcilable. There is a choice to be made between leaning on your strengths and compensating your weaknesses.

Following this same logic, according to Rolf, led Procter & Gamble to be patient with its agencies when they were doing badly but to show no hesitation in complaining when they were doing well. For P&G, and by definition, an agency that is in good shape never produces enough. This idea permeated all of Rolf's reflections; he had built up an idealized image of Procter & Gamble. One day he came into my office and said seriously: "P&G must have a problem: It has been at least a year since our last crisis." Rolf interpreted this as a bad sign; such calm could have meant that P&G was worried about the agency. In fact, I am pretty sure that P&G also puts pressure on nonperforming agencies. Yet this paradox had a great effect on me. I recognized that you have to be even more demanding when things are going well. You need to invest in your strengths.

I received my second lesson once again from Rolf. One day, no doubt exasperated by my stubbornness, he asked this question: "Do you want to be right or do you want to be president?" The question quickly turned into: "Do you want to be right or do you want to win?" I was not even thinking of becoming president yet, but I did understand what he meant. Despite its apparent cynicism, it made me think how the mania for being right, this typical French self-complacency, has little to do with business pragmatism.

The principle of there being one unique truth and multiple errors does not apply in the real world of business. If we can easily identify several roads to failure, it is no less rare for a single road to lead to success. There is no preestablished solution, independent of all else, that, should a manager discover it, would lead to him being seen as "right." At the risk of disappointing logical souls, I would say that success has little to do with being right.

This lack of understanding contributes to the ambivalence my fellow citizens feel toward business in general, and more specifically toward companies. In the book *Divorce French Style*, Hubert Landier explains that the French are convinced that chief executives "know everything" or at least that they "should know everything." The French people's defiance comes from the fact that they find it impossible to imagine that their bosses could feel the same uncertainties as they themselves. This fact goes to explain why "redundancies are perceived as a betrayal or an incompetence"; the French believe that bosses possess, or should possess, an element of truth that is inaccessible to mere employees. This perception of hierarchy reflects a deep misunderstanding of what a company is. Obviously, a chief executive does not know everything and cannot always be right.

So much for the French misconceptions about business . . . As a young man, I also became aware that it is not only illusory but also dangerous to try to predict the future. You just need to prepare for it, while staying flexible enough to deal with any eventuality and grasp any opportunity that arises. Of course, it remains crucial to anticipate problems and to deal with them before they get out of hand. Identifying potential risks does not, however, signify projecting yourself into the future or attempting to predict it. The future *per se* does not exist. It is shaped by a series of decisions taken by both the company and its competitors.

There is nothing new about this statement. Many companies have had experiences to confirm this. A few years ago, for example, the world was convinced that the printed book was living its final hours, and that people would soon be reading books in electronic format after downloading them from the Internet. The reality is that online bookstores sell tons of books over the Internet, but ship them out in their traditional format, that of the good old printed book, filling trains and trucks, while the e-book market has essentially failed to take off.

In the same way, Peter Drucker, the author of *The Age of Discontinuity*, reminded us in a recent article that the zipper was originally a system for closing cereal sacks, and was not intended for the clothing industry at all. A legion of such examples exists, starting with the Edison phonograph, which the fabulous entrepreneur and inventor initially created as a dictaphone for shorthand and which went on to revolutionize not only the music industry but music itself. Clearly, trying to predict everything is a futile exercise.

Because it is impossible to project ourselves directly into the future, I advised students not to be afraid of trying out different things at the beginning of their career, not to be afraid to fumble, change direction, and experiment.

There are vocational professions and then there are the rest. I envy those who have dreamed of becoming a doctor, an architect, or a lawyer from their earliest age. Most of them achieve great satisfaction as they get older. However, how many people have I met who were out of place? How many have made a decision one day and then, through hotheadedness, blindness, or simple obstinacy, persisted in the wrong direction? How many have taken one route and found themselves in a dead end? Each time I meet such a person, I feel as if I am experiencing real-life casting errors, tragic errors, that will follow them for their whole life.

I went on to tell the students that they should not hesitate to move from one activity or position to another at the beginning of their career. Doing so is a sign of lucidity, not instability. Before committing yourself, it is important to make sure you are on the right path. What we dare to do at the age of twenty five—change jobs—we may not be able to do at forty in such an audacious and carefree manner.

"You need to find what you love." These were the words pronounced by Steve Jobs during an inspired speech he gave to Stanford University students in June 2005. The founder of Apple explained that you should not hesitate to live several different lives. He added, "You will connect the dots"—in other words, it will all come together one day. To illustrate his belief, he described his last years at college. As he had no idea what he wanted to do with his life, he decided to stop wasting his parents' money and to drop out. After having slept on various friends' floors and worked odd jobs to survive, one day by chance he entered an amphitheater where a teacher was giving a typography lesson. Over the few remaining weeks of classes, he became an accomplished student.

By learning how letters and fonts are constructed, Jobs discovered a taste for beautiful things, something that inspired him when designing his first laptop computer, the Macintosh. He was seduced by the craft, even if he could not have imagined at the time that these few hours spent in a lecture hall, with no particular aim in mind, would have such an influence over his life.

"If I had never dropped in on that single course in college, the Mac would have never had multiple typefaces or proportionally spaced fonts, and since Windows just copied the Mac, it is likely that no personal computer would have them," Jobs said, then continued: "Of course it was impossible to connect the dots looking forward when I was in college, but it was very, very clear looking backwards ten years later."

In conclusion, I told the HEC business school students that unless they were already certain they wanted to become a corporate lawyer or an auditor, they should accumulate experiences. Doing so would help them to find the path upon which, one day or another, all of their previous experiences would come together. And I advised them to apply Steve Jobs's comment to their own lives: "Your time is limited. Don't waste it by living someone else's life."

COUNTERPRINCIPLES

A little later, I asked these same students what was, for them, the main role of a chief executive. Their responses came back as strategy, investment, and profit. One dared to suggest recruitment. Nobody gave me the answer I was looking for. For me, the main role of a leader is to bring clarity.

You need to take a position and then share it. This entails making sure that everybody understands what the company aspires to and, in consequence, that they are aware of its business model, its organizational structure, its major strategic directions, and its financial objectives. All of this must be written down and made very clear. Take Carlos Ghosn's second plan in Japan, Plan 180: to increase vehicle sales by 1 million, achieve 8 percent profitability, and zero debt over a period of three years. The objective could not be more clear and self-explanatory.

For us, as a network of companies present in so many countries, it is crucial to have a very clear set of objectives and strategies, and for them to be shared with everyone. The goal is for all of our ten thousand employees, without exception, to understand and adhere to the fact they work for a different kind of company. A company that does not only make ads, but also tries to propose disruptive strategies and that has a disruptive view of the world. This is exactly what we are aiming to achieve. It has resulted in the creation of a particular vocabulary (some business writers would call it "strategic vocabulary"), with all our people using the same language. We talk about Conventions and about Disruptions. Our project has been made clear for all, which is an essential condition for success.

I expected my audience to be surprised. Among the many functions of a manager, their professors had never mentioned the concept of *clarity* before. I continued in this same vein, presenting them with a series of principles, seven to be exact, that were rather surprising and certainly unconventional. Each principle goes against traditional management clichés. Each evokes the idea of Disruption. These principles make up our culture, which is why this chapter follows the preceding ones focused on culture and values.

After clarity, our second principle consists in refuting the idea that it is only strategy that counts. Hundreds of books since the 1960s have tackled the importance of strategy, with just as large a number of different definitions being used to describe it. The recurring theme is this placing of strategy above everything else, relegating execution to second place, considering it a trivial translation in the real world of noble strategic thinking.

We need to break away from this popularly held opinion. We love making intellectual speculations, we enjoy squabbling for ages over the basic values of this or that strategy. All managers want to be strategists; they consider it to be the most "noble" aspect of their job. Almost all. According to Carlos Ghosn, performance is determined much more by execution than by strategy. As a result, while he does not hesitate to set up committees to give birth to strategies, he ensures he is the sole pilot when it comes to controlling execution.

It is essential to accept that progress comes from focusing on what appears to be the least rewarding. To people wishing to enter the advertising business, I always explain that the first quality they will need is tenacity. Mere talent is not much use in the face of the countless obstacles that will get in the way of the best performance. Success is born of determination rather than just ambition. Ambition relates to strategy, whereas determination is linked to execution.

Our third principle concerns decision-making, and how to make it easier. As a general rule, the simplest decisions are taken without management even being informed. Only the most difficult decisions, those where the advantages and disadvantages of each solution appear to cancel each other out, to weigh equally on the scales, find their way up to the top management's desk. In this case, most of us only want to see the advantages and end up making decisions based on the positive aspects. Personally, I have always preferred to dwell on the negative consequences linked to any decision.

Do not hesitate to take the negatives head on; after all, you are going to have to live with them, once the decision has been taken. Thus, between all the negative aspects, you have to select those you prefer to deal with. Choice is driven by a combination of the capacity to solve a problem and the willingness to face it. In other words, not only do you have to be able to deal with the problem, you have to be able to want to.

Our fourth principle concerns error management. The right to fail is one of the most commonly used banalities in management books, which give it a much more important place than it merits. Though it is obvious, in my view, if you fail, you need to fail *fast*.

And it is not enough just to unearth the bad ideas quickly. They must be exposed. So many problems start small and become more and more important as time goes by because they have been hidden away. Contrary to the saying, bad news actually should travel faster than good news. Yet I know of few companies where the news travels in this way.

A fifth principle that is dear to us consists in cultivating incompetence. As Paul Arden, a brilliant British member of our profession, said: "It is better to live in ignorance than with knowledge. Solving the problem is the exciting part, not knowing the answer." Paul's formula is eloquent. I would not go as far as to recommend ignorance, but I would gladly suggest unlearning.

Because the future is not a simple extrapolation of the past, you have to know how to clear the decks and get rid of familiar ways of thinking to make room for new ideas. Two of our clients, Steve Wilhite, previously with Nissan, and Andrew House, from Sony, were invited to give presentations at Procter & Gamble training seminars. This is a far cry from *benchmarking*, a method that entails comparing every minuscule detail of companies within the same sector in order to measure yourself against the competition. Today P&G finds sources of inspiration within solutions from other industries. Its chairman, A. G. Lafley, recently declared that his main ambition was to turn P&G into a *learning company*.

We like this definition. As stated earlier, last year we created a Media Arts Lab in Los Angeles to gain inspiration from the creativity of our neighbors, such as Frank Gehry and DreamWorks. We learn more from other industries, because the effort involved in the transfer from one domain to another requires imagination.

Our next principle is about managing talent. Jack Welsh established a very tough rule at General Electric: Every year, each department head has to let go of 10 percent of his people—the poorest performers. This may not be too difficult to achieve in the first year, but imagine how hard it is if, by misfortune, you have been the head of the same department for five years.

Jack Welsh's way of doing things has infiltrated the culture of General Electric. It is not our way of doing things. We need to find our own way in order to attract and keep the best talent. Jim Collins, author of *Built to Last* and *Good to Great* has some good advice on the subject. This is what he said about talent management:

> Do not make plans and then look for the people. Do the opposite. Great companies first get great people on the bus, then decide where to drive it. If

you have the wrong people, it does not matter whether you find the right direction, you still will not have a great company. Great vision without great people is irrelevant. Conversely, if you have the right people with you, plans will set themselves up, moving forward. People come first. The "who" before the "what."

The more talented people are, the more the company needs to be able to take a step toward them. It is the company that needs to adapt. This is why I have often taken a stand against "job descriptions," or more precisely the importance they are given in selecting candidates. We have a principle—our sixth—which is to act differently and try to spot people who are interesting, sometimes atypical, different at least from what we initially had in mind. We establish the job description afterward. Put another way, we adapt the definition of responsibilities, even our organization and structure, to the salient elements of a personality. If the new recruit is truly talented, he or she has a right to expect the company to make a move toward him or her, within certain limits, of course.

This is why the interviewing of candidates, from beginners to the most senior, is an essential part of corporate life. I regret not having hired some of the candidates I have interviewed. I was not capable of giving them every chance to be at their best, to show their real potential. We would do well to be inspired by the likes of Bill Clinton. Each person who has had the opportunity of meeting him has said the same thing: "When you are introduced to him, it's as if you are the only person in the room."

Convince yourself that nothing is ever clear enough, do not try to predict the future, refuse to exalt strategy, treat the negative positively, fail fast, cultivate your incompetence, forget job descriptions—all of these are the principles, or rather the counterprinciples, that guide us on a daily basis.

But there is one more, the seventh of those that were given to the HEC students, and it is just as important: "We can be at the same time one thing and its opposite." Management is about reconciling opposites or, rather, going beyond them, transcending them. For over twenty years now, when I am presented with an arduous choice between alternatives, I know that the solution is often to be found elsewhere—not where you are looking, but in another place. In this way, I immediately agreed with Jim Collins' "Tyranny of the *Or*" concept. Thinking in terms of *or* forces us to choose between alternatives. Jim Collins invites us to consider the word *and* rather than be restricted by the word *or*.

Everyone knows that leading a company requires a permanent process of conciliation. But it should be conciliation without capitulation, which is the real challenge. Americans use the expression "balancing act" to define this capacity. It is needed throughout the life of the company.

We try to conjugate short and long term objectives, which means trying to overachieve in the short-term (even if this is tough), to be sure of having the means to invest in the long-term.

We try to balance organic and external growth, in the knowledge that few companies succeed in optimizing the rhythms of these two types of growth. Companies tend to be stronger in one or the other, according to their culture or where they are positioned in terms of their history. They have not necessarily realized that each of the two can multiply the effect on the other. As Jean-Paul Agon, the new chief executive of L'Oréal, said simply, "External growth is pointless if it does not contribute to the acceleration of internal growth."

We try to balance the continuously unstable relationship between global and local, between centralization and decentralization, in the knowledge that many companies suffer from swaying back and forth between these poles.

We try to find an equilibrium between knowing we can always do more with the employees we already have, which involves efficient recruitment methods and training programs, and the fact that whatever we do, there will always be a few with whom we will have to part company.

We try, in new product development, to decide on which ideas should come from within the company and those which could come from outside partners. Certain large organizations, such as Procter & Gamble, are already bringing in outside talent to develop a substantial part of their innovations.

We try to find the optimum balance between generalists and specialists, knowing that beyond the indispensable expertise of specialists, it is often the broader vision of generalists that creates the alchemy that adds the most value.

Finally, we try to reconcile our shareholders' rightful expectation of return on their investment and employees' rightful expectation of return on their efforts.

What is true of all professions is especially true of our own. Our business consists in bringing together notions that are often difficult to reconcile. For instance, in our industry, the key to creating effective messages relies on our capacity to link relevance and difference. It is easy to be different. A little less so to be relevant. It is difficult to be both at the same time.

It is interesting to note that Chiat/Day in America and our agency in France were the first to create a strategic planning department in their markets. We saw such a department as a place where rigor and imagination would meet.

There are so many apparently irreconcilable things to deal with. For example, we need to be capable of refocusing a brand, of capturing its essence, and, at the same time, of knowing how to stretch it out over the greatest possible number of products.

We need to know how to add value to mass-market products by upgrading them without forgetting for one moment the need to sell in quantity. At the same time, we need to democratize luxury products to give them access to the mass market without diminishing their aura. Each of these acts is contradictory; they are points of convergence that must be handled with finesse.

We need to work with external media-buying companies, which buy for several different agencies to create benefits of scale. But at the same time, we must retain audience experts within our agencies, people who can help the creative teams immediately understand the publics they are addressing and how to speak to them.

Every day we need to allow scientific and creative minds to work in tandem. And we need to find ways of combining the brio of expression with the solidity of content.

All of these notions have such different logics and perceptions that they would appear impossible to reconcile on a permanent basis. They often take the form of paradoxes, as a paradox expresses a form of contained tension. When you understand that you have to go beyond them, then you are able to shift the conversation, to place the thinking on another level, which leads you to immediately go further.

And you avoid unproductive discussions. You are no longer trapped in a sterile choice of alternatives.

At this point, it is "and," not "or."

* * *

I ended my presentation at HEC with one final observation. I pointed out to the students that those who have had the greatest influence on business, the great leaders of the last twenty years—Steve Jobs, Bill Gates, Jack Welsh, Lou Gerstner, A. G. Lafley, and Carlos Ghosn—have known how to *tame* change. They have made it so much their own that it has become second nature.

They do whatever needs to be done, whatever it takes. They drive the company forward, generate enthusiasm, and embody the source of energy on which employees thrive. It takes charisma to achieve all of this.

But like leadership, charisma is not necessarily innate. It can come over time; it can be developed. The six leaders I mentioned are more attractive today than they were twenty years ago. Both their personal and professional entourages would agree. They have become charismatic. Success makes you seductive.

PART III

Behaving Differently

9

The Advertising Man

(Or What Lee Clow Can Teach Others about Advertising)

I speak in this book of products, of brands, of the agency. It appears to me inevitable to also talk of the advertising professional. And naturally, I have chosen Lee Clow, the quintessential advertising man.

Few people are as genuinely charismatic as Lee. He has been described in many ways: a creative soul, the godfather of creative talents, a living legend, a guiding force, a professional agitator. A journalist from *Campaign* magazine in the United Kingdom even said that he felt, after an interview with Lee, that he was "in the presence of true genius."

As Alex Bogusky once said: "Advertising was one thing; after Lee, advertising was another thing."

I was once a creative director myself, coming from the client management department, which is quite an unusual transition. I nevertheless had won my fair share of Cannes Lions during the five years I was in the job. This part of my life gave me an insight into how difficult it is to be a great creative director. I had the chance of understanding from the inside the scope of Lee's achievements and how difficult it is to remain successful in this profession over a long period. In other words, as Lee said: "Everyone can have a great 'moment in time,' but to try to sustain it over a career and agency history is a very difficult challenge."

Lee likes ideas. He believes that ideas rule the world. They accelerate change. They make him vibrate, they enthuse and sometimes move him. No one more than he knows how to recognize them. He can see them before they even really exist. One or two words, a rough sketch of a visual, and he can imagine the beginnings of an idea. Some people need to see the whole idea, the finished campaign, before being able to make a judgment. From almost nothing, Lee detects something, however small, that he will contribute to making big.

One of my French colleagues once said: "An idea is something that we have the desire to remember." I like this evocation of desire as an influence on memory. This is how advertising works. The unexpected creates the desire to be remembered. And this is why Lee always comes with fresh thoughts and cannot accept anything that looks déjà-vu.

Lee is a gatherer. Nothing pleases him more than to see a team working successfully. He loves pinning medals on others. While he gladly assumes responsibility for everything, he is most happy when others receive the accolades. And now and then he likes to remind them: "Don't take your work seriously, take it passionately."

He does not know the meaning of the word "jealousy." Or "envy." This makes him a very rare species in his community. How many times have I heard him rave about the merits of a new campaign by Dan Wieden, Jeff Goodby, or Alex Bogusky? "Who did that?" is his favorite question . . . Lee just loves great work.

Management by walking around is no secret for him. He is always in motion. He moves from one office to another, gives advice in the conference room, stops in front of a poster layout, sits in on a brainstorming session where he will suggest some concepts for an upcoming new business pitch, goes back into his office, strokes his dog, and finally calls his colleagues who cannot wait to come and join him in his tiny office.

He so enjoys strolling around that he has built his offices to make it easy to do just that. Entering the Los Angeles office makes your creative expectations rise by several notches. This is as true for his clients as for his people. Everybody feels unconsciously inspired.

In fact, our agency in Los Angeles is difficult to describe. From the outside it is nothing more than a huge rectangular box. I was told it used to be a helicopter hangar. Once inside, however, it becomes an incredibly deconstructed space, like a collage in three dimensions. There is a tree house, an indoor park called Central Park, and a basketball court. The creative teams' offices are bright yellow metallic units that are arranged like a giant construction game. Some departments have huge tents that break up the open space. Others sit along Main Street, where a vintage Datsun station wagon is parked. The surfboards it carries on its roof reminds us that we are in California.

It is quite the opposite of a *jardin à la française*, where symmetry and right angles rule. In L.A., walking around is an unpredictable experience. What you have just seen does not foretell what you are about to see. But somehow it all makes sense. It has just been thought differently. It is probably as close as you get to what a great creative mind looks like. Lee's mind, undoubtedly. Free, brave, beautiful, simple, and inspiring.

Lee is also the ultimate Californian. He loves his home state because natural optimism reigns. It is a place where people are passionate about new ideas. And this is because California is the nexus where so many of the media arts converge—from music, to the movie industry, to Silicon Valley, to the video game industry, and to what we do for a living. Lee's opinion is shared by Jacques Attali, one of the most renowned French essayists, who sees Los Angeles as the capital of the world after Bruges, Venice, Amsterdam, London, Boston, and New York. He wrote in his last book *Une Brève Histoire de l'Avenir (A Brief History of The Future)* the following on the surge of California: "Everything changed the year a young man named Steve Jobs launched the first personal computer. Los Angeles became the new capital of the world. And it still is today." It is striking to note that Attali chose the launch of the Apple computer as the symbolic date of the swing of influence from New York to California. Even more so because Steve Jobs, the Macintosh, and the launch campaign of 1984 are omnipresent throughout this book.

Talking about Apple, the iPod campaign will always be remembered as iconic and . . . very simple. What makes Lee so special is his gift to simplify what appears complicated. In the end, everything is summed up in one or two words, sometimes three: *Done, Think Different, Shift, Impossible Is Nothing, Dogs Rule* . . .

Having great ideas is one thing; being able to preserve them is another. One of Lee's less obvious but essential qualities is his stubbornness, his refusal to concede or compromise. For the past four years he has wanted to change the packaging of a product of one of our international clients. He has never given up, and keeps coming back to the subject. Over time, he has become more obstinate. After all, he worked for nearly thirty years with Jay Chiat, who said to him every day: "Always disappointed, never surprised." You need to have character to be able to cope with a comment like that and never give up.

Lee Clow's contribution to our industry is clear and indisputable. No one better than he has known how to express the essence, the soul of a brand. Product benefits or features have never been his passion, contrary to an Ogilvy or in certain ways a Bernbach. Lee knows how to *shape* brands and to make sure that these brands enjoy a larger share of the market than they could even have imagined. He feels almost instinctively what a brand can become. In fact, Lee loves brands, those brands that are honest and respectful of consumers. He holds brands in the highest regard, and he demands that we all, clients and agency, constantly strive for the higher ground. Nothing is worse for him than to underestimate a brand and what it could become.

There have been, and still are today, other great creative people elsewhere in the world, but no one has ever known better how to use *media arts*, as Lee calls the world of communications, to design the brand. He considers advertising as an art form and advertising people as sorts of "artists." I mean, of course, street artists such as Toulouse-Lautrec, whom Lee likes to cite as an example of a man who decorated the streets with his art when he invited people to visit the Folies Bergère.

To quote Lee: "I have always felt the word 'advertising' is either a diminutive or derogatory term that kind of goes with stuff people don't like, and I always felt frustrated because I felt like I was a communication artist or a media artist. The best advertising is one of the art forms of our culture."

Disruption is what brought all our agencies together. It has become the backbone of our company. I believe Media Arts is what will move us to the next level and make our company one of the most interesting companies in our industry.

Most art directors are not very talkative. But when they do express themselves, they often use flowery, metaphorical language. Lee is no exception to the rule. He speaks slowly, his words weigh heavily, he affects the heart as well as the mind. But he also knows how to be economical with words. The few sentences that he put together to describe Disruption are the perfect example:

It's more than a noun. It's more than a book. It's more than a process. It's a way of thinking.

It's a way to look at our clients' business and find opportunity.

It's a way of defining how brands should act.

It's how each of our agencies should do business every day.

Think boldly. Sell brave ideas. Create dramatic business results for our clients.

Disruption means dismantling the status quo and replacing it with something bold and new.

It can be the most powerful thing we sell.

It can be what the world expects us to do.

It can define who we are.

One day Lee thought that TBWA should have a backward slash after the name. TBWA\. It was his way of showing that TBWA\ is the great facilitator, the go-between that has allowed all Chiat/Day, Hunt/Lascaris, and BDDP agencies to group together. The back-slash became the company's symbol in the same way that the abstruse squiggle that represents Disruption. Here is what Lee said:

Technology has conquered geography.

More and more, the Big Ideas of the future will be global ones.

TBWA, the brand, will join us together as a family in the new century.

It will become known for harnessing the power of ideas.

Ideas of all shapes and sizes.

Ideas that change our clients' business.

Ideas that change the way advertising networks work.

Ideas that redefine creativity.

Ideas that make the best talent in the world want to join us.

TBWA will not be the typical agency network strangled by layers of multinational management. The slash represents a global creative community, born from a shared vision and a shared passion of the world's most renowned advertising agencies.

We rejoice in diversity.

We grow on the single-minded promise of delivering clients

a larger share of the future.

United we can shift paradigms, redefine categories and rock industries.

Here comes the next century. It's time to change the rules.

It's time to disrupt.

One of our former managers, responsible for our largest New York–based client, was previously a senior partner in one of the leading management consulting firms. He came to the conclusion that the best problem solvers were often advertising agencies, agreeing with Lee when he says: "Consultants only do dissection of companies." The analyses agencies make are both accurate and insightful. More often than not, the solutions, the campaign ideas, even the brand ideas they propose crystallize everything. A few words or a few images can change the way you see a problem, can sometimes even move mountains. For me, Lee is the ultimate problem solver. I am not sure that he would appreciate this description. But it truly is the final result of his interventions. When advertising is powerful, it changes fortunes. Ask Energizer, or Apple, or Adidas . . .

Bringing original solutions to resolve problems requires us not to be afraid of creating a bit of chaos. For Lee, "good management" can lead to complacency. We think we have done the right thing because we have done it right. Lee thinks we should create chaos—but not planned chaos—as a part of a management process. *Real* chaos, where we cannot imagine beforehand what the final consequences might be. And this is why he adopted Disruption as soon as he came across it.

For three decades, Lee has attracted into our company a number of great creative minds, those people whose talent shapes who we are and what we do. They form a unique worldwide community that does not reflect society such as we know it, with its restraints, burdens, and frontiers. It is a community that is never satisfied with things as they are.

All the major agencies have dreamed of bringing together such a community at one time in their history. Lee has made this dream a reality and given all the great creative people working for him the energy to go further. I would like to say a few words about three of them, or rather quote them. Their talent makes us stronger. Their words strengthen our culture.

The first is John Hunt, our worldwide creative director, whose contribution to our company has been immeasurable. This is what he says when he speaks about Disruption. It is something Lee could very well have said himself on the subject:

> We were sold from the very beginning. This way of thinking allowed us to understand our very selves. Our unorthodox behavior had a name. There was real preparatory thinking behind it. We felt justified, legitimized.

Lee is truly disinterested. Only *ideas* interest him. Here is what Erik Vervroegen, the creative director of TBWA\Paris and the world's top creative award winner for the past few years, has to say concerning "désintéressement":

> If I have a secret, it is this: money and power are not appealing to me. I'm completely and absolutely free in what I do and because I think this way, I'm still a child in my mind. I don't want to lose that, I really do not want to lose that. That's why I don't own a house. I don't have anything. My life's just in a bag and that makes me a good creative person, because I'm afraid of the future.

Lee has often said: "Big ideas win. Good ads don't." Rob Schwartz, the creative director of TBWA\Chiat\Day in Los Angeles and world-wide creative director for Nissan, commented:

> A good ad is a moment in time. It is finite. But a big idea is eternal. A big idea can create good ads, but more importantly, a big idea can organize and inspire a company. It can move a culture.

* * *

Tom Carroll, our worldwide president, jokingly calls Lee and me the "two hippies." It is true we both turned twenty during the 1960s, we bought the same records and were probably both attracted by the same anti-establishment culture. May 1968 was a hot time at both Berkeley and the Sorbonne.

I do not know about myself. I am afraid I have changed a lot. But Lee has remained true to himself. It is a fact that hippies go about business hoping that they will one day change the world. It may sound naïve but it has left an indelible mark on us . . . And Lee has always tried to make things move.

The Brand

(Or Why Companies Should Think of Themselves as Brands)

Questioning what we think we know, strangling old clichés, going against the grain—these are the keys to successful marketing. The smartest brands have always acted this way. Some have even gone further by making an anti-establishment stance the very theme of their communications. *Shift*, the slogan of Nissan, *Impossible Is Nothing*, the mantra of Adidas, and *Think Different*, the signature for Apple, all have this in common.

To outmaneuver IBM, and subsequently Microsoft, Apple certainly needed to think differently. To overcome the giant that Nike had become, Adidas convinced itself that impossible was nothing. To contest Toyota's leadership and Honda's dynamism, Nissan forced itself literally to shift the way it operated.

When a new campaign appears on the walls or on our television screens, the first people to take notice are the company's own employees.

When done right, advertising creates an internal groundswell. Staff confidence increases, and the energy of the sales force along with it.

The employee at Apple who has personally always strived to *Think Different* sees a poster on the company walls with those very words validating his way of being. The new product designer working at Herzogenaurach, headquarters of Adidas in Germany, pushes himself to propose the most innovative of products, because the brand's advertising reminds him every day that *Impossible Is Nothing*. The engineer at Nissan asks himself if the new project he is working on reflects the spirit of *Shift*. He wants to know if it truly represents a big enough change in terms of what already exists in the market.

"THINK DIFFERENT"

We are fortunate to have as a client a truly visionary leader with an extraordinary talent for imagining the future. Steve Jobs has been the initiator of three separate revolutions: the personal computer with the Macintosh, online music with the iPod, and mobile communications with the iPhone. Not one revolution, not two, but three. Almost nothing is a surprise coming from Steve Jobs. He has built up a company culture that allows talented people to create unique products and invent technologies that change the world.

For a revolution to be total, to become cultural, the public needs to be ready for the change. Apple has succeeded each and every time. At each turning point, the product was different, radically in some cases, such as Apple's move from computers into music. Each time the company was faced with a new environment. And each time it created different ways to stir up public interest and initiate a new cultural movement. In 2001 with the iPod, in 1997 with the iMac, and in

1984 with the Macintosh, ruptures were created, what we call Disruptions.

Thirteen long years separated the 1984 and the 1997 revolutions. Thirteen years that saw Steve Jobs's departure from the company— dismissed at the age of thirty, by the chief executive he himself had appointed. Thirteen years that saw the company tremble as a result of strategic errors and disappointing products.

When Steve Jobs took back the reins of the company, even his core customer was asking if Apple was not about to finally fade away into the background. It was vital to convince those still loyal to the company to keep the faith; they had to believe in the future of Apple once more, and be reminded of what the brand really stood for. At the same time, it was urgent to restore the company's founding culture from the inside, to revive its pioneering spirit. It was a vital step in giving birth to a new wave of revolutionary products.

These products were not even ready when the campaign was set to launch. In reality, one of the key advertising goals was to gain time. The *1984* spot announced the imminent arrival of the future. In 1997 Apple's future was still being shaped, but it could be seen on the horizon, and Apple management wanted to prepare the territory. "To do this," said Lee Clow, "we had to reach back and find the soul of the company once again."

From the outset, Apple has attracted people who go against natural convention. Perhaps not a huge client base, but one made up of *influencers*. A club of iconoclasts, open-minded intellectuals, people who make things happen. For them, their computer was more an extension of their own self rather than a machine. It allowed them to do, to create, to dare. It made people realize they were more creative than they had thought. Apple increased self-realization by revealing a person's full potential. In a word, Apple did not make business machines, but tools for creative minds. The agency decided that the most relevant way to express this message was to celebrate creativity itself.

The *Think Different* spot is the well-known black-and-white documentary that brought to life a gallery of iconoclasts, including Albert Einstein, Bob Dylan, Martin Luther King, Muhammad Ali, Maria Callas, Mahatma Gandhi, Alfred Hitchcock, and Pablo Picasso. The actor Richard Dreyfuss delivered the voice-over:

> Here's to the crazy ones.
>
> The misfits.
>
> The rebels.
>
> The troublemakers.
>
> The round pegs in the square holes.
>
> The ones who see things differently.
>
> They're not fond of rules
>
> And they have no respect for the status quo.
>
> You can quote them, disagree with them, glorify or vilify them.
>
> But the only thing that you can't do is ignore them.
>
> Because they change things.
>
> They push the human race forward.
>
> And while some may see them as the crazy ones, we see genius.
>
> Because people who are crazy enough to think that they can change the world,
>
> are the ones who do.

From the small screen, the campaign quickly conquered the outside world: posters, murals, and buses carried portraits of the personalities who appeared in the spot. No text accompanied the images, nor was any reference made to the product, just two words: *Think Different*.

The ads were impossible to miss in the major cities of America. Larger-than-life celebrities appeared even bigger when displayed across enormous billboards. The campaign became a hot topic of discussion with people asking each other: "Have you seen the one with John and Yoko?" Some portraits even fueled debates around certain personalities, such as the Dalai Lama, Gandhi, and César Chávez. They were not the types of people we were used to seeing in advertising.

People living in France will remember a fifteen-yard-wide photo of Picasso posted on the southern wing of the Louvre. Not every face was necessarily recognizable to everyone. The youngest among us may have asked who the face belonged to when seeing a picture of Maria Callas, but they did know that the answer was worth finding out. The campaign provided food for thought, which kept the phenomenon alive.

Think Different allowed Apple to reclaim its place in popular culture before it had even launched one product. Steve Jobs once said that this theme serves as a rallying cry at Apple. Here is what he told representatives from his industry about his company values at the time of the launch of this film, in 1997:

> Those people that are crazy enough to think they can change the world are the ones that actually do. A lot of things have changed, but values and core values, those things shouldn't change. The things that Apple believed in, at its core, are the same things that Apple really stands for today . . . And so, we wanted to find a way to communicate this, and what we have is

something that I am very moved by. The theme of the campaign is Think Different. It's the people honoring the people who think different, and who move this world forward. And it is what we are about, it touches the soul of this company.

Think Different. These two words hang from the walls of the company headquarters, to remind the troops that "this is who we are, and this is what we do every day at Apple." At the same time, the campaign renewed investor confidence and reassured worried Apple customers who questioned whether the brand they loved would be able to live up to its promises. The world was now ready to accept what Apple had to offer. It was good timing: The product in question was extraordinary: the iMac.

A few years later, at a time when Apple appeared to have shaken up the world of computers once again, its management was already thinking in a new direction. In 2001 the company launched the iPod, which would quickly become the standard in the MP3 player market. And by launching the iTunes Music Store in 2003, allowing easy and legal downloading of digital music at a modest price, Apple practically reinvented the music industry.

Once again, just as with *1984*, Apple defied the system and changed the world. But the revolution sparked by the iPod was even more deep-rooted. It had a different scope. If the computer is part of many people's lives, music reaches out to everyone. As a computer manufacturer, Apple was a cult. Music has transformed it into a club that the whole world is invited to join.

The iPod films were born from the idea that dance is a common language to all music lovers. The agency launched a search for great, unknown tracks. The bet paid off; B-sides became overnight hits and previously unknown artists international stars. The *New York Times* observed: "Its beats have made the iPod a new way of living within which digital is king . . . without a word, the ads present the viewer with a choice: shake it and be part of the movement, or be sadly left behind."

Films featuring U2, Eminem, and Wynton Marsalis came next. Thanks to an advertising spot, this jazz musician's album exploded the sales figures of jazz successes of the last fifty years. A track by Rhinôçérôse, a niche rock band from Montpellier in the south of France, would be the soundtrack to another spot. Just a few days later, the group signed up for a Japanese tour. As for Bob Dylan, he saw his latest album shoot to the top of the American music charts. He has not enjoyed such success since the launch of *Desire*, thirty years earlier. The commercial in which he is seen singing a song from *Modern Times* was highly instrumental in this renewed commercial glory. As a journalist from *Advertising Age* explained, his deal with iTunes helped Dylan even more than Apple.

Not only are brands being endorsed by celebrities; celebrities are now partnering with brands like Apple to reach publics previously out of their reach. The conventional commercial logic has been reversed.

The opportunities for Apple today appear limitless. The digital revolution will surely take on original and new directions. We have already seen a woman run up, sledgehammer in hand, to smash a screen projecting the rantings of Big Brother; we have seen Picasso, Einstein, and Gandhi appear together, side by side, in the same film; we have seen shadows dance in a contagious manner; and we all know that more unexpected things are yet to come.

I wrote these lines hardly a year ago. Since then Apple has continued to create new initiatives, such as literally bringing computers to life by using two beautifully cast actors to personify the PC and the Mac. This has become the most famous side-by-side campaign of the last ten years. Bob Garfield of *Advertising Age* summed up the spirit of the campaign: "In humiliating Microsoft, Apple's simply charming."

And then came the new revolution: the iPhone. As this book is going to press, it is too early to talk about its success. So far, only one commercial has been run: at the Oscars, showing stars answering the phone with a variety of "Hellos." The stars go from Lucille Ball and Jerry Lewis, in black-and-white clips, to Robert Redford and John Travolta, from more recent movies.

Once again Apple has exploded the barrier between advertising and entertainment. Once again Apple is launching a revolutionary innovation. Once again Steve Jobs has imagined a very seductive product. Once again Apple is paving the way.

"IMPOSSIBLE IS NOTHING"

A brand can be famous without people truly knowing anything about it. They can know what a brand does without understanding what it represents. They see the label or logo without necessarily knowing that behind this symbol lies a story, a precious heritage and an enduring passion.

This is the case for a brand that many of us have grown up with: Adidas. Legendary athletes such as Mohammad Ali and Jesse Owens have worn its sports shoes and sportswear. The 1960s were its glory years. Then gradually the brand became bogged down through the frequent changing of shareholders, losing its luster. The time had come to bring back its competitive spirit, to rediscover this state of mind that had made it accomplish things that had never been dared before.

At the beginning of the 1950s, the founder of the brand, Adi Dassler, was at his most inspired in striving to achieve the "impossible." He invented a shoe with studs that prevented soccer players from slipping on wet turf. The shoe was specially designed for Germany's national soccer team, of which Adi was an ardent supporter. In the World Cup final, Germany faced the Hungarian team, the absolute favorites, led by the stars of the era, Ferenc Puskás and Sándor Kocsis. Adi Dassler's shoe turned out to be the secret weapon of the Mannschaft, the German team. On a rain-sodden, slippery pitch, Germany became world champion, bringing a ray of hope to a nation at war with itself in this painful postwar period.

The Adidas name would subsequently be associated with numerous other champions and sporting legends in search of the "impossible." It was while wearing Adidas footwear that Mohammad Ali created a name for himself and became the revered champion we all know. Nadia Comaneci achieved perfection in women's gymnastics dressed by Adidas. Pete Maravich and Kareem Abdul-Jabbar revolutionized basketball while wearing Adidas.

The turning point for the brand came at the beginning of the 1990s. At this point, Nike had taken the lead and imposed its own marketing rules, turning sporting events into a very expensive form of entertainment. Nike laid down its rhythm overnight. Sports marketing would favor a glorified few, and the best athletes would become stars.

Adidas had a different kind of culture. Unlike Nike, Adidas supports all athletes at all levels. The shoe with the three stripes ran on the cinders of suburban athletic fields. Adidas bucked conventional wisdom, which says a brand should choose the two or three sports that are the most interesting from a commercial point of view. Instead, Adidas became involved in each and every type of sport. However esoteric. Its employees share a common love of sport in general: A beautifully executed banana kick in soccer excites them as much as a slam-dunk or a hail-Mary pass.

Its glorious past and rich heritage did not save Adidas from confronting a difficult challenge: Today's youth is not necessarily interested in sporting history. The task was to bring the brand spirit into the modern world, linking the past with the present, even the future, and in a relevant way.

The idea that has bridged the gap between today and yesterday is that of the "impossible." Trying to achieve the impossible has always been a motivating force. Is it not the desire, deep down, of athletes to achieve what had never been done before that motivates them? You could take away the prizes and the advertising contracts, and there would still be someone trying to jump higher, run faster, to throw farther, or score more points. The true athlete is not discouraged by the impossible. Quite the opposite; the impossible is an irresistible challenge.

In the presence of Mohammad Ali and Laila, his twenty-eight-year-old daughter and women's middleweight boxing champion, we launched the following manifesto in Harlem:

> Impossible is just a big word thrown around by small men who find it easier to live in the world they've been given than to explore the power they have to change it. Impossible is not a fact. It's an opinion. Impossible is not a declaration. It's a dare. Impossible is potential. Impossible is temporary. Impossible is nothing.

This text was printed on a thirty-foot-high poster carrying large photos of the two athletes, on the corner of 125th Street and Malcolm X

Boulevard in New York City. We created a large number of films around this idea, beginning with one starring Ali and his daughter.

We see Ali in a huge arena, in the era of the famous fight that saw him confront George Foreman in 1974 in Kinshasa. The voice-over begins as he gets into the ring. We see his adversary, the hood of his cape pulled down so far that we cannot make out the face. A few moments later we discover that it is Ali's own daughter.

The bell sounds and the fight begins. As in 1974, Ali dodges each punch that his daughter throws at him. After several fruitless attempts, she finally manages to hit his face. Ali loses balance, slightly taken aback. A few moments later he smiles at Laila through slightly gritted teeth. As they return to their corners, she gives him a knowing grin, which he answers with a wink.

This time the voice-over is given by Laila:

> Impossible isn't a fact. It's an opinion.
> Like when they said it would be impossible to beat Sonny Liston.
> He's too powerful, too experienced.
> Or when they said don't take the fight in Zaire.
> He's too young, too strong, he's gonna destroy Ali.
> So when my father looks impossible in the eye
> And defeats it, again and again
> What do you think I'm gonna do when I hear people say a woman shouldn't box ...
> Yeah that's right.
> Rumble young girl, rumble!

A towering basketball player walks the streets of San Francisco. As he waits for the light to change, he invites a passerby to climb on to his shoulders . . . then a second and a third. A frenetic race involving all sorts of people ensues, with people even jumping from the rooftops to be part of what is now a human pyramid. The basketball player continues to walk on without difficulty, a pair of Adidas on his feet. He smiles. He is carrying the whole world on his shoulders.

The film's opening shot is of a young Latin American boy. He stares up into the sky and snatches a plastic bag blowing in the air. Various scenes follow that lead us to understand that the young boy is trying to collect as many bags as possible, going so far as to rummage in trash cans and even "borrowing" one from a homeless person. He goes to an empty building site, sits on the ground, and starts to put the bags together. We gradually realize that what we thought was a boy collecting bags to earn some pennies was in fact him making a soccer ball, which he starts to juggle skillfully. Perhaps he will one day become a soccer star, having started out like his idols in the underprivileged areas of his country.

Each of these films, like the tens of others we have produced, highlights the campaign theme in its own particular way. *Impossible Is Nothing* speaks to every person who, whatever his age or status, sees sport as a personal challenge, a passion, a competition against oneself.

This is what Eric Stamminger, chief executive of the Adidas brand, had to say in a speech to his managers: "For each and every member of the Adidas family, Impossible Is Nothing, this attitude, this philosophy has become part of our daily lives and our language. The impossible has never existed in our brand's history and never will in our thinking. It's our legacy, our mission and our challenge."

Impossible Is Nothing truly raised the company's spirits. It renewed confidence in the brand and urged employees to believe in it even more. Salespeople in the United States now feel more confident taking on Nike. Designers do not hesitate to ask stars like Stella McCartney to conceive amazing new collections. Shoe developers are now imagining new models filled with revolutionary technology.

As Ulrich Becker, international communications manager for Adidas, pointed out, "We were looking for a way of expressing our attitude toward the brand that was really involving and capable of generating strong emotion. It so happens that this is exactly what *Impossible Is Nothing* is doing."

"SHIFT"

Yokohama, September 2004. Carlos Ghosn takes one determined step toward the podium. Japan is watching him closely. Over the last few years, Ghosn's success in piloting Nissan, which was on the brink of collapse when he arrived, has made him a national hero. The press has applauded his astonishing results. In three years, sales have leapt by almost 1 million vehicles. In 2004, Nissan was the most profitable company in its industry, with debt wiped out and share value increasing fivefold.

But this extraordinary resurrection went above and beyond mere commercial success. It took Carlos Ghosn audacity to shake up a revered local company, defying detractors and traditionalists who had warned him he was walking on eggs. Open to ideas and influences from all over the world, he was conscious that it is sometimes just as important to defy conventions as to respect traditions, and he has been the forerunner of a new era in Japan's economy and culture.

Since his arrival in 1999, Carlos Ghosn had made giant leaps forward. But everything seems to point to this being just the beginning. On September 2, 2004—the date chosen by Nissan to present a new model range—everyone was asking himself what he would do next.

The tension reigning over the Ohsanbashi Hall in Yokohama, where the event was held, spread to Tokyo. The hall was bursting with journalists and spectators. Giant screens were set up in the nine largest cities in Japan, allowing the general public to follow the head of Nissan's speech. Thousands watched him shake up old habits once again.

That day he would present a total of six new models all at once, something never seen before from a Japanese auto manufacturer. This market initiative was accompanied by a surprising speech. In particular, the first word he pronounced on reaching the gallery struck everyone.

"Shift." A single word that captures the passion and commitment that have revived Nissan, and drive our future. Everything we touch, we shift; and everything we shift, we try to make better, and uniquely Nissan.

What does the notion of Shift signify for Nissan? In changing our way of thinking, we change the way we look at things, the way we act, the way we react to what is going on around us. It's more than Kaizen; it's no longer about just doing, but doing for the purpose of driving better, faster, higher performance ... Shift is who we are, and how we work. It is a challenge to each employee, each supplier, every day, to reexamine how they work, and how they can create more value for our customers.

The choice of the word *"Shift"* goes back several years. The agency had been brought together to discuss the brand's image and how long it would take to evolve it. We knew that in the automobile sector, the perception of models can progress rapidly. But the image of the brand, which comes from the accumulation of the images of the models, takes longer to improve. Customers may be quite happy to buy a Maxima, but are not yet proud to own a Nissan. The gap between product and brand is much wider than in other sectors. There is much more inertia.

We had created a brand film for Nissan in the United States two years earlier, showcasing each new model, where the voice-over concluded: "A shift can change a person, a life, the world . . . or it can simply change the way you move through it." And so *Shift* became our slogan. Each vehicle launch since has been signed "Shift": the Murano with *Shift Convention*; the Maxima with *Shift Exhilaration*; the Pathfinder with *Shift Adventure* . . .

Two years went by. Over time, we realized that *Shift* was more than just a slogan. Carlos Ghosn demonstrated this in a spectacular fashion when he began his speech in Detroit in February 2004, six months before the Yokohama speech, with the two soon to become famous sentences: *"Every time we look at something, we shift it. And every time we shift it, we try to make it better."* *Shift* evoked the idea of a company looking to see things differently, from a different angle and a new perspective.

Because the translation from one language to another makes the formula lose part of its appeal and strength, the word "Shift" has remained in English in practically every country, including Japan. The same is true for *Think Different* and *Impossible Is Nothing*.

Shift has become the key word for the company, and Nissan Tokyo headquarters has adopted it worldwide. It has become a truly global concept, which is a first in the automotive industry. *Shift* encapsulates everything that Nissan stood for in its glory days: Its employees have changed the course of automobile history with major innovations since the company's creation in 1916. It is worthwhile noting that the term "shift" appeared in certain documents distributed by Nissan but the agency did not know about it. Interestingly, the word achieves its full potential when it refers to what the company has become over these last few years since Carlos Ghosn took the reins, driven with his desire to challenge everything.

It summarizes all that Nissan wants to communicate to the people working for and with the manufacturer. In a book published in the United States—aptly called *Shift*—Ghosn described his experience and also explained how he is far from being satisfied with Nissan's impressive results. "I am proud of what we have done," he said, "but I am not happy with where we are." Nissan's new philosophy forbade all self-satisfaction. Never again would it settle for the status quo.

We know we are doing our job well when our most senior clients appropriate our advertising slogans within their own speeches. Steve Jobs explained the concept of *Think Different* to the computer distributors that are his clients. Erich Stamminger claimed that *Impossible Is Nothing* to an enthusiastic audience of Adidas employees. Carlos Ghosn refers regularly to *Shift* in motor show presentations from Tokyo to Detroit.

In each case, articulating a big and defining brand idea helps to change the way a company thinks of itself. It provides a unifying vision and rallying cry that propels the brand forward. And, by referring to these ideas, our clients use advertising to show to the world how they themselves see their companies.

* * *

What we have seen with Apple, Adidas, and Nissan also holds true for the vast majority of the companies whose campaigns have been described in this book. They refuse the established order and understand that failure to change is fatal. To succeed, or simply survive, they know that it is not enough simply to rely on their past success, nor is it enough to entertain the illusion that the future is a mere extension of the present.

"You can never bathe in the same river twice," states one of the oldest paradoxes known. The future is not smooth. It can only be reached by a series of ruptures, very rarely through continuity. Nothing endures but change.

Conclusion

"The best is yet to come." This is always my answer when I am asked about the future of our industry.

Throughout this book, I wanted to evoke the horizons opening up before us, the unexplored paths that we are going to take, the unexpected mountains we will climb. I have insisted that, from now on, creativity will no longer be an option. It will be mandatory.

The generations we are talking to understand even the subtlest of our intentions. Our children can guess marketing strategies even before they have been written. The power has shifted into their hands. Today's consumers control the marketplace.

We have to earn their attention.

In these lines, I wanted to share how our agency has been preparing itself to meet this new challenge. We are in battle order. We have developed Disruption, because we believe that no one, be it ourselves or our clients, can grow without regularly challenging the course of action. And we have turned Media Arts into a craft to bring creativity to every meeting point between a brand and its audience.

Finally, we are fortunate to work for clients who want to follow us, or sometimes even precede us, up the steep paths ahead.

There is a sense of adventure in the course our agency has taken over the past few years. But we all feel that this is nothing compared to what the future holds. A future inhabited by ideas that are simply waiting to be imagined.

It is only the end of the beginning.

Index

Acknowledgments

Thanks to Nick Baum, without whom this book could never have been finished. He counseled me, corrected, and accompanied me throughout its completion.

Thanks to my partners at BDDP, Jean-Claude Boulet, Marie-Catherine Dupuy, and Jean-Pierre Petit, without whom much of what is written in this book could never have taken place.

Thanks also to the account leaders who have allowed the great campaigns described in this book to exist. I am thinking of James Vincent, Tom Blessington, Jean-Marie Prenaud, Anne Vincent, John McNeel, Corey Mitchell, Mike Allen (and our friends of 180), and not forgetting Robert LePlae, who has led most of the people mentioned above.

Thanks to my assistant, Rosanne Le Roy, who has coordinated my work and provided me with precious advice.

Thanks to Laurie Coots, for her continuous support, and to Brandon LaGanke, Clément Leonarduzzi, and Nicolas Dalibard, for the desk research they had the kindness to perform.

Thanks to all my friends throughout the network who, in one way or another, have added their touch to this book. In particular, Emmanuel André, Nicolas Bordas, Tom Carroll, Fiona Clancy, Alastair MacLean, Iona Macgregor, Rod Wright, and Jonathan Ramsden.

Thanks to Akira Miyashi, Ichiro Zama, and Ayami Nakao Pelata for their understanding and friendship.

Thanks to Séverine Barraud and Claire Burgess, for all their suggestions, which, from page to page, have given more substance to this book.

Thanks to Pierre Nora and Olivier Salvatori, who have supported this project from the outset.

And finally, thanks to Airié Stuart, my editor, for the confidence she has shown me.